Spiritual Values
in
SHAKESPEARE

Spiritual Values
in
SHAKESPEARE

Ernest Marshall Howse

ABINGDON PRESS
New York *Nashville*

SPIRITUAL VALUES IN SHAKESPEARE

Copyright MCMLV by Pierce & Washabaugh

Library of Congress Catalog Card Number: 55-6074

SET UP, PRINTED, AND BOUND BY
THE PARTHENON PRESS, AT NASHVILLE,
TENNESSEE, UNITED STATES OF AMERICA

FOREWORD

UNIVERSITY students have formed a substantial proportion of my three congregations: Beverly Hills Community Church (Presbyterian), California; Westminster United Church, Winnipeg; and most of all, Bloor Street United Church, Toronto.

Keeping in mind the interests of students, I have periodically employed sermonic themes which could be reinforced from classical literature.

On one occasion, a sermon illustrated by George Eliot's *Romolo* brought an inquiry if I would deal with some of Shakespeare's plays. The challenge provoked an experiment which grew into several series entitled *Parables in Plays*.

Most of the series dealt with contemporary plays, but, because of the student request, the trial effort was made with four tragedies of Shakespeare. These, combined with a later Shakespearean series, form the basis of the chapters in *Spiritual Values in Shakespeare*.

My design is to make the vividness of drama present and illuminate timeless human passions, and to reveal how the integrity and insight of a great master have at times transformed the changing scenes into parables of unchanging truth.

ERNEST MARSHALL HOWSE

5

111624

CONTENTS

7

[1]

DRAMA
Religion's Prodigal Daughter

ENGLAND," said Victor Hugo, "has two books: one which she made; the other which made her—Shakespeare and the Bible." [1]

We need not agree with Hugo's nineteenth-century rationalism—"faith excommunicates imagination"—to agree with his insight into the enduring influence of these two books. Shakespeare and the Bible must be reckoned among the formative influences in English literature and in the life of English-speaking peoples.

The two volumes are more than complementary. Shakespeare has been called the secular Bible, but he is not merely secular. As the most casual reader can discover, he is saturated with the language of scripture. He may have known little Latin and less Greek, but, like Bunyan later, he knew one book— a book which had never been printed in English until his own day.

Shakespeare did not have the King James translation, which has been so pre-eminent since his time. The King James translation appeared in England in 1611, the year in which Shake-

[1] Victor Hugo, *William Shakespeare* (London: Hurst & Blackett, 1864), p. 312.

speare completed his final play, *The Tempest.* But this "author-
ized" version took fifty years to become a popular favorite.
In all probability Shakespeare, like the pilgrim fathers who in
1620 brought their Bibles to New England, used the cherished
Geneva version. In any event he would find in the version he
used the cadences of Tyndale and Coverdale, and he was in-
spired with their majestic music. He knew the Bible so well that,
in hundreds, indeed in thousands, of his passages we can trace
its phraseology, and beyond its phraseology we can trace its
thought.

Shakespeare is not the gospel as the Ten Commandments are
not the gospel, and, indeed, as many of the parables of Jesus,
in themselves, are not the gospel. Yet though Shakespeare can
in no wise be counted a Fifth Evangelist, he does deal with the
verities of a moral universe; and he displays in his poetry that
"stretching of the soul in wonder and amazement" which has
been a timeless characteristic of great religious literature.

Alfred Noyes says that Shakespeare in his attitude toward
the moral law shows everywhere the influence of Christianity,
that he had a capacity for thought and emotion, a breadth of
charity and humanity, that were not possible to Greeks and
Romans. In many a passage, such as that on the quality of mercy,
we can trace the passing of

> those blessed feet,
> Which fourteen hundred years ago were nail'd
> For our advantage to the bitter cross.
> (*Henry IV,* Part I, Act I, scene 1)

In short, Shakespeare was speaking in a voice that could only
sound at the period of the Renaissance and the Reformation,
when, as it has been finely said, Greece rose from the dead
with the New Testament in her hand.

This is not to say that we can take isolated passages from

10

Shakespeare's plays and quote them as expressing Shakespeare's belief. In his last will and testament Shakespeare wrote: "I commend my soul into the hands of God my Creator, hoping and assuredly believing, through the only merits of Jesus Christ my Saviour to be made partaker of life everlasting."

If such was his faith, it is folly to try to deduce it from the mouths of his characters. Shakespeare is far too great a dramatist for that. Only in the sonnets, says one, does Shakespeare enter the confessional. In the plays—except, perchance, *The Tempest,* in which all the characters are unreal—Shakespeare himself does not speak. He lets the characters speak for themselves.

For example, one may want in praise of wine to quote Shakespeare: "Dost thou think, because thou art virtuous, there shall be no more cakes and ale?" or to produce Iago's argument about "a good familiar creature." Another may reply, "O thou invisible spirit of wine, if thou hast no name to be known by, let us call thee devil. . . . O God, that men should put an enemy in their mouths to steal away their brains!" None of the quotations has more the authority of Shakespeare than the others.

A possible clue to Shakespeare's own judgment lies in the character of the person who thinks such thoughts. What kind of person produces the plea for drink? It is Sir Toby Belch, perhaps the most disreputable character in Shakespeare's gallery. What kind of person speaks of men putting "an enemy in their mouths to steal away their brains"? It is Cassio, a gallant, intelligent soldier who has seen that drink has been the instrument of his ruin and the thief of his reputation—the immortal part of himself.

The distinction, however, is frequently not so simple. In Shakespeare's plays good and evil, strength and weakness, are so subtly intermingled in the same character that we are baffled by the complexity. Shakespeare knew, as Browning, that

11

Evil or good may be better or worse
  In the human heart, but the mixture of each
Is a marvel and a curse.[2]

Shakespeare, then, is no moralist; yet morals are his stock in trade. We can find no consistent body of principles running through the plays, but as we watch, we can see the whole range of human experience "shot through with heaven and hell." He never points a lesson, but, as Alfred Noyes says, his apprehension of reality is profoundly that of a soul aware of the eternities.

It is strange, therefore, that there has been such an unfortunate antipathy between pulpit and stage, and that the pulpit has given so small a place to Shakespeare. Too many Christians seem to have minds resembling that of Caliph Omar, who destroyed the great library of Alexandria on the grounds that the books must either be in agreement with the Koran or in contradiction; and that if the first, they were needless, if the second, reprehensible. A more discriminating concern for scriptural truth might have shown us that the "oceanic" and "myriad-minded" genius who gave us the tragedies has illustrated with unparalleled power the deepest lessons of the Book of life.

Before we deal specifically with Shakespeare, we shall look back through more than two millennia to discover the source wherein the river of great drama begins its flow. That far-off spring we shall find issuing from the sacred places of faith and worship.

The prototype of every stage performance was the dancing and acting of long-forgotten tribes as in primeval scenes they prayed for sun and rain and a harvest that meant nothing less than life itself. The passage of time brought the great outdoor

---

[2] Robert Browning, "Gold Hair."

temple of Dionysius with choruses and dances in honor of the god of vegetation. As the festivals continued, the proportion of music and dancing decreased, and the proportion of speech and story increased. Slowly the pattern developed until the great poets of Greece were presenting dramatic performances to audiences numbering twenty thousand.

The long process progressively discovered the scope and fashioned the form of drama. Poets gradually gave increased importance to the chorus. Aeschylus introduced the second actor, added dialogue to monologue, and opened the possibility of dramatic action. Sophocles introduced a third actor and the use of scenery. Euripides brought the action from the conflicts of the gods to the natural passions and affections of men and women.

As the poets toiled in the creation of their new art, they learned the different factors which would play upon the emotions of an audience: conflict, suspense, choice, climax, solution. And as the spectators watched, increasingly they saw not only an acted story, but also new lights on ancient problems of crime and punishment, sin and forgiveness, and—even in Grecian plays—some new insights into the redemptive power of suffering.

Philosophers thought on the issues of life and said: "Do you *follow?*" Poets thought and, in their drama, said: "Do you *see?*" The audience did see something that could not well be said— and went away, having had their spirits refreshed, their hearts exalted, and their imagination set aflame. Drama began in religious experience and at its best has retained, throughout all stages of its development, something of that experience.

If we turn from ancient times to seek the source of modern drama, we must come again to the places of worship. We must come to medieval England with its villages and towns where the dwelling houses centered around the church. Mass was said in Latin, but most people did not understand Latin and, indeed, could not read or write in any language. So some resourceful priests, eager to convey the Christian evangel, resorted to ancient religious strategy and began to present truth in drama.

The first attempts were merely simple pageants of the religious festivals. At Christmas there would be presentation of the scenes at the birth of Jesus, the visit of the shepherds and of the wise men, and the massacre of the innocents. As scenes were presented, the choir would sing. (The first sound effect of the modern theater was a church choir.) At Passion Week the trial and death of Jesus would be presented. And at these festivals the crowds who could understand no word of the Latin Mass, who had no Bible and no religious literature, and who, indeed, for the most part were totally illiterate, flocked to the church to *see* the acted stories and legends of their faith. Modern drama began as a technique in religious education.

Before long the simple pageants of Christmas and Easter developed more complicated forms, and some churches began presenting stories from the Old Testament and episodes from the lives of the saints. In time, plays developed into three standard types: the *mystery* play—not a "who-dun-it," but a portrayal of scriptural incident teaching Christian truth; the *miracle* play, an episode in the life of a saint; the *morality* play, with a theme such as mercy, charity, forgiveness. The modern drama, as the ancient, came to birth in the festivals of religion.

At first these plays were presented in the chancel, but as they grew in popularity, the crowds became larger than the churches could hold, so the plays moved outside. They were presented at the entrance of the church. The first stage of the English play was a platform in the doorway of a cathedral. The next stage, literally as well as metaphorically, came when someone had the idea of putting the platform on wheels to roll it away. Before long someone else had the idea of rolling it to some other location and presenting the play to a different audience. The word "pageant" means "rolling platform."

As the platform rolled away from the church, the plays moved away from their original purpose. They lost their sense of mission to the human spirit. The religious element declined and the secular, and soon the vulgar, ascended. As the wagons arrived, not at the church, but at the market place, tradesmen capitalized on the gathering. They put up booths and stalls, and the place began more and more to resemble not a religious festivity but a country fair. In due course the tragic element was replaced by the comic. The themes were still for the most part religious, but now the shepherds were more concerned with a sheep stealer than with the angels, and Noah's wife caused more trouble than all the other animals in the Ark.

Hamlet told his players: "There be of them [clowns] that will themselves laugh, to set on some quantity of barren spectators to laugh too, though in the mean time some necessary question of the play be then to be considered: that's villanous." (*Hamlet,* Act III, scene 2.) The caution was a suggestion of something more important. The stage had been concerned with great issues, but the audience wanted amusement—often crude amusement—and the actors gave them what they wanted.

The next development was inevitable. Some smart innkeeper saw the gatherings which congregated at the place and knew their capacity for thirst. So he built a permanent stage next to his inn and invited the traveling actors to present their plays upon it. In return for trade the actors lived on the house. The theater began to get softer. The players did not have to think about their wagons getting stuck in the mud, and because the stage was permanent, the spectators who were able to pay could be provided with seats. The temptation was too strong.

In a short time the rolling wagons disappeared. The permanent stage was built, though still *outside* the inn; and the theater was born.

To survey the whole development: religion in ancient times gave drama its birth; religion at the coming of this modern age gave drama its rebirth; religion created drama, nourished it, imbued it with dignity and purpose; and drama grew up to be religion's prodigal daughter.

A generalization never tells the whole story. Many factors influenced the development of drama. In England there was a change in culture. The Elizabethan Era brought a new national spirit. Young writers grew up with a new sense of freedom and struck out on new paths in the development of literature. In the glorious years of Marlowe, Jonson, and Shakespeare, drama soared suddenly to a peak, only to fall into decline and degeneration from which it did not recover till the time of Ibsen. Indeed, that first peak of dramatic achievement reached an altitude not since surpassed. The great plays which Shakespeare produced at the height of his career deal with the issues of human life, not for an age, but for all time.

The following chapters, however, will not be an academic course on Shakespeare, a dose of "Shakespeare without tears." They will have limited use for the classroom. They will not raise any issues about Shakespeare's existence. They will not enter the lists against the student who declared that the plays of Shakespeare were written not by Shakespeare but by some other man of the same name. They will not mention Bacon, save to quote his essays. "When I get to heaven," said Mark Twain to Chauncey Depew, "the first thing I am going to do is to find out Bacon and ask him who wrote Shakespeare."

"But," said Depew, "suppose Bacon isn't in heaven?"

"Then," said Mark Twain, "you ask him."

These chapters also will avoid many other issues which rise like apparitions through the fog of academic discussion. A German play represents Goethe reincarnated as a college student. The great master in his lowly guise has to take an examination on himself, and he fails to achieve a respectable standing. He does not even remember incidents which the examiner seems to consider of supreme importance, and his opinion is often directly counter to the dictum of accepted texts. Were Shakespeare reincarnated, he would probably be equally bewildered by many of our textbook discussions, and by the casual assumption (made by experts) that only experts can understand what he said. *The Christian Century* printed this immortal gem:

> I dreamed that William Shakespeare's ghost
> Sat for a civil service post.
> The English paper for that year
> Was on the subject of "King Lear."
> William answered rather badly—
> You see he hadn't read his Bradley.[3]

The picture is intriguing. Think of poor William biting his pen and scratching his head, baffled by the demand that he explain *King Lear*. How could an amateur like Shakespeare be expected to know much about Lear? What could Shakespeare make of some of the academic analyses of his plays, dealing in such esoteric terms as Oedipus complex, overcompensation, inferiority complex, and agitated depression?

In some classrooms of our modern world, Shakespeare would certainly be puzzled by interpretation. One critic assures us that Hamlet, being a disguised woman in love with Horatio, could scarcely help seeming unkind to Ophelia. Another says that Hamlet, a very clever and wicked young man,

---

[3] Reprinted by permission of *The Christian Century* from the issue of January 5, 1949.

faked the ghost to oust his innocent uncle from the throne. Shakespeare would have sympathized with Arthur Bradford when he said: "I am more or less happy when being praised, not uncomfortable when being abused, but I have moments of uneasiness when being explained." [4]

We shall, therefore, not proceed with the analysis of plot and counterplot; we shall, rather, watch the stage and *see.* As we see, we shall realize that though the highest cannot be spoken, it can be acted. We shall find that even though the plays are not what we call religious plays, we are in an atmosphere essentially religious.

Religious drama, it needs to be said, is not by any means limited to drama designed for production in cathedrals. It may be produced entirely for the secular stage. It may not have a biblical theme—certainly it need not resemble *Salome* in one direction nor *Green Pastures* in another. It may have nothing to do with good-natured priests with an Irish brogue, attractive nuns from Protestant Sweden, or hard-bestead clergymen living with *One Foot in Heaven.* And it may have no resemblance whatever to the weak sentimentality of *The Passing of the Third Floor Back.* It may not mention God or Christ; indeed, holding the mirror up to nature, it may even deal with something sordid or evil. Yet it may be genuinely religious.

The essential marks of a play with religious value are to be found in the kind of choices that are presented, the quality of insight that is revealed, and the stature of the life that is portrayed. Often drama may contain nothing specifically biblical and yet be of the very texture of Christian thought, so that it would be impossible to imagine its being produced save in a culture influenced by the Hebrew prophets and Jesus.

With even wider reference, if the drama reveals (even amid

[4] Quoted in *The Christian Century,* January 5, 1949.

the muck) some eternal quality, so that the audience finds something true, beautiful, and good, so that it sees life, however marred, not as contemptible but as infinite, holding "large discourse, looking before and after," then, in the ultimate sense, drama is religious. It has what Lorado Taft said is necessary to give greatness to sculpture and, indeed, is necessary to give greatness to any art, the "hint of Eternity."

Fred Eastman tells us that some years ago when one of O'Neill's plays was being presented in New York, a spectator remarked as he left the theater, "It's so good to get out into the Depression again." The plays of Shakespeare are not so. They are indeed full of realism. They are not success stories. They have no happy ending. They do not end up with poetic justice. Who does not wish that Juliet might live, that Lear and Cordelia might be happy, that Desdemona might find in her marriage the rich rewards that her beauty and faithfulness deserve? Shakespeare did not write it thus. He presented the world as it is. The purpose of his plays was: "To hold as it were the mirror up to nature, to show virtue her own feature, scorn her own image, and the very age and body of the time his form and pressure." Shakespeare, therefore, presents cruelty, injustice, iniquity. Yet even amid the gloom of evil deeds the inherent grandeur of the soul shines with unfading glory. The spectator always sees something in the spirit of man which tragedy does not conquer but ennobles. Says Bradley: "Shakespearean tragedy is never, like some miscalled tragedies, depressing. No one ever closes the book with the feeling that man is a poor mean creature. He may be wretched and he may be awful, but he is not small. His lot may be heart-rending and mysterious, but it is not contemptible. The most confirmed of cynics ceases to be a cynic while he reads these plays." [5]

[5] *Shakespearean Tragedy* (London: Macmillan & Co., 1949), p. 22.

19

We may see goodness vanquished, but our hearts are on the side of goodness. We may see evil victorious, but we loathe it even in its victories. As George Morrison says, we leave the plays of Shakespeare "with the glowing certainty that the good are the real victors though they perish and that heaven, though dark with clouds, is on their side." [6]

With this brief prologue we shall now raise the curtain successively upon a series of eight Shakespearean plays. We shall open with four tragedies, *Hamlet, Othello, Macbeth, King Lear.* Then we shall turn to four other plays—three of them, *Richard the Third, Julius Caesar,* and *The Merchant of Venice,* written prior to the tragedies; and one, *The Tempest,* written after, as the curtain call of the departing master. As we watch, we shall learn the truth in the observation of an English philosopher that drama as it transcends the language of words in the language of action becomes "one of the most powerful instruments ever invented for conveying the highest truths to the human mind." [7]

[6] *Christ in Shakespeare* (London: James Clarke & Co., 1928), p. 39. Used by permission of the publishers, James Clarke & Co. and Harper & Bros.
[7] L. P. Jacks, *A Living Universe* (London: Hodder & Stoughton, 1924), p. 24.

[2]

HAMLET
The Tragedy of Indecision

MORE HAS been written about Hamlet than about any other character in English literature. For generations literary celebrities have found a favorite indoor sport in dissecting the Prince of Denmark; and when they have taken him apart, they have cheerfully refashioned him nearer to their heart's desire. There are as many different Hamlets as there are different critics. There is the romantic Hamlet of Goethe; there is the Coleridgean Hamlet of Coleridge; and it has recently been discovered that Hamlet was the original Existentialist. "We should be thankful," wrote T. S. Eliot, "that Walter Pater did not fix his attention on this play." [1]

The significant fact is that all the critics have some of the truth, and none of the critics has all the truth. Hamlet has so much good and evil, so much strength and weakness, so subtly intermingled that, after all our examination, he remains an enigma. And there is little hope that I shall now complete the restoration of his shadowy portrait.

Hamlet is to literature what the "Mona Lisa" is to art. (Some time ago when I was thinking of *Hamlet*, this reference to the

---

[1] *The Sacred Wood* (London: Methuen & Co., 1948), p. 99.

21

"Mona Lisa" leaped without lineage out of the vacancy which is called my mind. Later, when looking at T. S. Eliot's essay on *Hamlet,* I was surprised to read: "Hamlet is the Mona Lisa of literature." [2] Perhaps a man may have a certain joy in discovery even when he discovers only the principle of the wheel.) Those who have seen the original know that they can never quite fathom what goes on behind La Gioconda's eyes. The man who stands before her is never sure how much she is saying, "Come," and how much she is laughing at him for coming. He can never with confidence read the meaning of her smile.

We can never read quite clearly the character of Hamlet. It has been well said that no actor is ever good enough to play the part of Hamlet until he is too old to be able to play it. One thing is sure: Hamlet is an authentic personality. Bone of our bone and flesh of our flesh, he is, in the phrase of Lewis Carroll, "as large as life, and twice as natural." Everyone who watches with insight the course of the play will find himself saying—as, indeed, he will at some point in *Macbeth* and *Othello* and *Lear*—not only, "There, but for the grace of God, go I," but also, "There am I." The purpose of the play, it may be put, is that having been read, it may read you.

The play was not an original creation. It was an old Saxon story which had already been cast in a succession of plays. In certain places Shakespeare does little more than revise the language of a previous playwright. Shakespeare probably felt, as Josh Billings did later, that originality in literature was played out and the best thing any man could do was to steal with discretion.

It would be tempting to assume that the play is universally familiar, and that the "gentle reader" can be confidently ex-

[2] *Ibid.*

pected to recall any important character and any pertinent reference. Perhaps the assumption may be a trifle optimistic.

A script writer wished one of his characters to say, "Man does not live by bread alone"; and another to reply, "Oh, yes, Genesis"—or whatever the book happened to be. As the writer did not know, he sent an inquiry to the research department of his network. The library sent back a reply locating the original source of the quotation: "Man does not live by bread alone—not even pre-tested bread," from *The American Character* by Denis William Brogan. The incident is a revealing indication of the mental atmosphere in which bright young minds of today are being brought to bloom.

Hence, for the convenient refreshing of all memories, and for the particular aid of readers to whom Hamlet made his last appearance from behind the covers of a compulsory text, I shall begin by presenting the story in bare outline.

In Denmark the king, Hamlet, has been murdered by his brother Claudius. Before the murder Gertrude, the king's wife, has been the mistress of Claudius; and now in indecent haste she marries him, and he supplants on the throne the rightful heir, Hamlet, Junior. The young Hamlet meets the ghost of his father, who tells of the "foul and most unnatural murder," and, in the fashion of the time, demands immediate vengeance. Hamlet proposes obedience, but his introspective nature makes him dilatory. He counterfeits madness to escape suspicion that he could be any danger to the usurping king. Others, seeing the young man act as though half crazy, make the most obvious deduction and conclude that he is in love. Hamlet has previously courted Ophelia, the daughter of Polonius, the lord chamberlain. Her father now instructs her to give Hamlet what in modern slang is called "the brush-off."

Hamlet seems to be annoyed at Ophelia's inconstancy and changes the honey policy to the vinegar policy.

Hamlet tests the ghost's story by presenting before the usurping king a play reproducing the circumstances of the murder. The king, seeing everything he has done faithfully re-enacted on the stage, realizes that Hamlet knows his guilt and immediately plans to have Hamlet sent to England on a mission in which he will be killed. Meanwhile Hamlet goes to his mother and violently upbraids her for having married his father's murderer. He hears a noise and, thinking that the king is spying, swiftly thrusts a sword through a curtain and kills Polonius, the father of Ophelia. Hamlet is now sent to England, but pirates capture his ship and return him unexpectedly to Denmark. He finds that Ophelia, her weak mind disordered by her successive sorrows, has perished by drowning, probably by suicide, and that her brother, Laertes, is home to take revenge for the death of his father.

The king determines to employ Laertes' anger to rid himself of Hamlet. So he arranges a duel between the two. Laertes poisons the tip of his sword, and, in case that fails, the king poisons the cup of wine from which Hamlet will drink to refresh himself. In the duel Laertes wounds Hamlet, but is himself cut with the same poisoned sword. Knowing that nemesis has overtaken him, Laertes then tells Hamlet what the king has done. Hamlet thereupon uses the poisoned weapon for one last thrust at the king. Gertrude, Hamlet's mother, has meanwhile drunk the poisoned wine—at hand to cheat Hamlet even of victory—and the play ends in somber Shakespearean fashion, strewn with corpses and dark with tragedy that might have been averted had Hamlet displayed the native hue of resolution. As the curtain drops, one remembers the couplet:

Oh, the little more, and how much it is!
And the little less, and what worlds away! [3]

The story is a poor one—in spite of adultery, a mad woman,
a fight in a grave, and eight violent deaths. But Shakespeare
did not need much of a story. Here, as elsewhere, he uses the
story simply as an operating table on which to dissect human
character and to show what ruins and what ennobles the lives
of men and women.

Let us then observe, though in fashion all too meager, some of
the things that meet us in the play.

When the ghost appears to Hamlet to reveal the murder,
Hamlet says at once:

> Haste me to know 't, that I with wings as swift
> As meditation or the thoughts of love,
> May sweep to my revenge.

He speaks as a man of action, and all through the play he per-
forms as a man of action. He is not effeminate. He is an expert
swordsman. He does not lack courage. He insists on following
the ghost and, when others would have shielded him from
danger, says: "By heaven I'll make a ghost of him that lets
[hinders] me." He is the first to leap on board the pirate ship.
He draws a sword and uses it when he thinks someone is spying
upon him. He swiftly seizes the chance to use the players. He
can suit the action to the word. At the last he wins a warrior's
tribute and the finest eulogy in Shakespeare:

> Now cracks a noble heart. Good night, sweet prince,
> And flights of angels sing thee to thy rest!

Hamlet can be vigorous in action, that is, so long as the

---

[3] Robert Browning, "By the Fireside."

action comes immediately upon impulse. He is a man to whom second thoughts are not best. To him second thoughts are always treacherous. Whenever he begins to debate his action within himself, the river of his intention runs into the sands of introspection.

In "The Hollow Men," T. S. Eliot has paraphrased such experience:

> Between the idea
> And the reality
> Between the motion
> And the act
> Falls the Shadow
>
> .   .   .   .
>
> Between the conception
> And the creation
> Between the emotion
> And the response
> Falls the Shadow.[4]

The play sets forth the deadly consequence of flight from needed action to indecisive reflection. No man, it is true, can escape inner conflict; as Browning later said:

> When the fight begins within himself,
> A man's worth something.

But no man can safely remain divided within himself. Only a person integrated to the degree that he does not consume all his energies in inward struggles can effectively meet outside difficulties. Reflection must at last clear the way for action. A man may think that he cannot decide, but he will find that indecision too prolonged means that he has decided, perhaps in the worst of all possible ways.

[4] *Complete Poems & Plays* (New York: Harcourt, Brace & Co., 1952), p. 58. Used by permission of the publishers.

Had Hamlet swept on to his revenge, the king would have been killed. The king was killed anyway. Hamlet was at last driven to the justice he could not choose. But consider the price of delay. Polonius is stabbed, Ophelia is drowned, Laertes is killed in the duel, Rosencrantz and Guildenstern go to their doom in England, the queen is poisoned, and in the pentecost of calamity Hamlet loses his own life. Of the eight who died, seven might have been saved had Hamlet followed his first intention. Hamlet presents, not, as Macbeth and Othello, the tragedy of headstrong passion, but rather the *tragedy of insufficient passion*. Shakespeare lets us see that this can be equally calamitous.

Why did Hamlet delay? asked a question in an English examination paper. A coed answered, "Because if he had acted, the play would have ended too quickly." That may be a dramatic reason. Let us observe some others. Significantly, Hamlet himself could not have said why, when he had cause and will and strength and means to do it, he did not act. He said himself, "I do not know." Macbeth was perfectly aware why he followed his line of action. Othello knew too well what spurred him to his tragic deed. But Hamlet, more intelligent than either of these, was, like many intelligent people, unable to understand himself.

The observer looking at the play from the outside can see certain threads moving consistently through the tangle.

First, it is clear that no matter of conscience was involved concerning the pattern of private vengeance. We must not import into that ancient time the conscience of the twentieth century. Hamlet would no more think it wrong personally to avenge his father than we would to call a policeman. There was no shadow of guilt in taking action. There was guilt only in doing nothing. He questioned, "To be, or not to be," but never, "To do, or not to do."

Again, the tragedy was not due to circumstance. Aeschylus and Sophocles presented fate, not human weakness, as the essential factor in a play. A flaw in the structure of chance destroyed Oedipus—not a failure of virtue. In the older play by Thomas Kyd, *The Spanish Tragedy,* of which Shakespeare made use, the delay was caused by the difficulty of assassinating a monarch surrounded by generals. But in *Hamlet,* as indeed in Shakespeare's other tragedies, circumstance is not an essential factor. Toynbee in his *A Study of History* remarks that as Shakespeare moves from the lower to the higher levels in character scale, he shifts the place of circumstance farther into the background. The primitive character of Henry V is revealed, in part, by the challenge in the human environment about him. But circumstance means less in *Macbeth,* and in *Hamlet* the scope is narrowed entirely to the internal conflict in his own soul. The scope of action is within the surging spiritual forces which this one personality holds within itself.

In a dozen different places Shakespeare took pains to show that Hamlet could have had his will. His popularity was such, and the king's unpopularity such, that at any moment Hamlet could have swept the usurper from his throne and finished the stern act of justice. Indeed, the king was afraid that even Laertes might do as much. In two soliloquies Hamlet reproached himself bitterly for the neglect of his duty, but even to himself he never pretended any external difficulty. The crux of the drama lies not in any outward pressure of propriety or circumstance but in some flaw within personality. Wherein then shall we trace the soul's tragedy?

We must begin with the essential emotion of the play. Unmistakably this is the overwhelming disillusionment which had come to Hamlet concerning one he loved—his mother. He had seen her apparently devoted to his father, hanging on him

> As if increase of appetite had grown
> By what it fed on.

He had seen her following his body to the grave, "like Niobe, all tears." And then within a month ("O God! a beast . . . would have mourn'd longer"), he had seen her marry her husband's brother, a man entirely contemptible. Oscar Wilde spoke of the widow whose hair had turned quite gold from grief. Hamlet saw his mother equally shallow and behaving in a fashion which he could interpret only as a surrender to coarse sensuality. He did not know that before his father's death she had been his uncle's mistress; but he could not fail to see that all he believed in her was suddenly and terribly destroyed.

Our modern psychologists (most of whom do not begin to plumb the human soul as deeply as Shakespeare does) know well enough that our sense of security and integrity in the universe is to a deep degree the reflection of the security and integrity of our home. It is a profound spiritual hurt to a youth to say with loathing he cannot control, "Would it were not so!—you are my mother."

When Hamlet's faith in his mother was so brutally shattered, his whole world was shaken to its foundations. After that, it just did not seem that anything mattered. And that first shock was augmented by another. Not only had his mother failed him, but the woman he loved had also failed him. Ophelia was a pretty thing, partly by nature and partly by art. Hamlet looked at her and said, "God hath given you one face, and you make yourselves another." But if Ophelia was pretty, she was also treacherous and unworthy of confidence. She lied to Hamlet, and he guessed as much. He looked into her eyes and said, "Are you honest?" and,

29

reading her correctly, he answered, "No." Then he added, "Get thee to a nunnery." That, he thought, was the only place for such human putty.

Ophelia was indeed a weak thing for a time of struggle. She had no strength to cope with difficulties. True, she lost her father and her lover, but many women have had to face these trials. Ophelia crumpled under them. She came to her wit's end— apparently no great journey. We can summon no excessive pity for her even in her madness. When she dies, a suicide, we feel not so much regret as relief.

One feels how different life might have been for Hamlet could he, at a time of great distress, have turned to some Cordelia or Portia or Desdemona, to some woman he could believe to be worthy of all confidence. George Morrison says that negatively Shakespeare shows what an infinite loss it is to a man never to have loved a woman who by her own excellence has called forth his best.

What happened to Hamlet is what happens to many. When a youth loses faith in one person around whom his life is centered, he is apt to lose faith in everything. One person is shown to be a sham; and the moral foundations of the universe sink in bogs and quagmires. Blue glasses may seem a small personal thing, but for the one who wears them they can make the world look blue. Hamlet felt that if his mother could deceive him, deception might be everywhere. He had been so hideously tricked that he could trust nothing. If his mother had been the impersonation of a lie, why not also the ghost? Perhaps the spirit he saw was the devil tricking him further. After Hamlet lost faith in his mother, there was always doubt, always uncertainty, always cynicism. Here lies the essential emotion of the play.

This central emotion, however, is not in itself sufficient to explain the tragic defect in his character. There is something else underlying it and preceding it. T. S. Eliot in his excellent essay on the play says that Hamlet is tormented by an emotion that is inexpressible because it is "in excess of the facts." Hamlet, he says, is up against the difficulty that his disgust is occasioned by his mother, but that his mother is not adequate cause for it. His disgust envelops and exceeds her.[5]

With deference to Mr. Eliot, I would suggest that though the emotion is in excess of the facts as relating to the mother, it is not in excess of the facts as relating to Hamlet's own life. From the beginning of the play something is wrong with Hamlet himself. When he appears on the stage, he is already sick of life, heavy with the blighting disease of youth, world weariness. Already he looks upon all the uses of the world as "weary, stale, flat, and unprofitable." "This goodly frame, the earth," for all its "majestical roof fretted with golden fire," appears to him no other thing but "a foul and pestilent congregation of vapours." "On the earth nothing so pathetic as man himself." "What a piece of work is man! how noble in reason! how infinite in faculty!" yet but the "paragon of animals," the "quintessence of dust."

> Imperious Caesar, dead and turn'd to clay
> Might stop a hole to keep the wind away.

"Now get you to my lady's chamber," he says as he looks at the skull of Yorick, "and tell her, let her paint an inch thick, to this favour she must come; make her laugh at that."

The spectacle of the man just murdered merely serves to remind Hamlet that "a king may go a progress through the guts of a beggar." "Man delights not me," he says. We are but "fools of nature . . . with thoughts beyond the reaches of our souls."

[5] *The Sacred Wood* (London: Methuen & Co., 1948), p. 101.

Bradley says that Hamlet brings to us the sense of the soul's infinity. He also brings to us the sense of the soul's tragedy. Hamlet does nothing because nothing is worth doing. In his own revealing phrase, "It is no matter." Nothing matters because in the world there is no sense; nothing without corresponds to the great feelings within. No eternal justice answers our cry for justice. We are indeed the "fools of nature . . . with thoughts beyond the reaches of our souls."

I suggest, then, that the disgust and loathing, the settled weariness in Hamlet, though, as Eliot says, in excess of the facts created by his mother's deeds, is not in excess of the facts created by his own thoughts. It is not in excess of the facts of any life whose ultimate reading of the universe is that of Hamlet's.

When Thackery wrote *Vanity Fair,* he said, in a letter to his mother, that he wanted to portray the emptiness of people living without God in the world. In *Hamlet,* Shakespeare has shown us (perhaps as unconsciously as D. H. Lawrence and Ernest Hemingway in this generation) the same emptiness. *Hamlet* is not a religious drama. There, indeed, lies its unconscious power. But *Hamlet* reflects the tragedy of all persons who find themselves "fools of nature . . . with thoughts beyond the reaches of our souls." The tragedy of Hamlet is not that of a puny man at war with God; nor even that of a man at war with society. It is, rather, that of a man at war with himself, in a world where there are no values worth the struggle.

All this, though indeed in excess of the dramatic limits, shines through the play. All this Shakespeare portrays simply by portraying life in the ultimate solitariness and loneliness of the individual without any relationship to God. All this is portrayed without dealing with religion, without pointing any moral, and yet with such perfect fidelity to the unchanging experience of life that when we see the curtain drop after a great performance, or close the book after a quiet reading, what Hamlet said, as words without thought, we are moved to say with humble feeling

> For my own poor part,
> Look you, I'll go pray.

OTHELLO
The Tragedy of Jealousy

THE FIRST tragedy which Shakespeare wrote after *Hamlet* was *Othello*, and the two, though seeming to be worlds apart, have striking similarities. In both we see the effect on a soul of sudden and overwhelming shock—the shock of losing faith in a loved person around whom the life is centered. Hamlet felt the shock of losing faith in his mother, Othello of losing faith in his wife. It matters not that in *Othello* the cause is spurious. The clear point of the tragedy is that the consequences are as real as if the cause were real.

In *Othello* we are reminded again how intimately our faith in life and goodness is intertwined with faith in some person in whom the deep trust of our life is centered, and concerning whom we feel, as Othello did of Desdemona, "If she be false, O, then heaven mocks itself!"

As wise surgeons of the soul have so often found, the bitterest atheism may be but the projected emotion from the shattering of a child's confidence in father or mother, or a grown person's in husband or wife or some intimate friend greatly trusted. To lose faith in such a person is often to make uncertain all the sanctities of life.

OTHELLO: *The Tragedy of Jealousy*

Othello has one difference from the other tragedies. The passion, the action, the interest all lie strictly within the sphere of domestic life. Sex plays but an incidental part in *Hamlet, King Lear,* and *Macbeth;* it is central in *Othello.* Perhaps for this cause *Othello* has a more close and intimate hold on the common interests of our time.

In *Othello,* as in the other tragedies, Shakespeare began with a familiar story. "The Moor of Venice" was an old Italian tale, simple and sordid enough, concerning the unfaithfulness of wives and husbands. It dealt with the eternal triangle—the married life where three is company and two is none. Shakespeare wove the magic of his genius through that old story and transformed it into "the subtlest of tragedies, the most pathetic of human compositions." Let us, then, turn to the story, the skeleton underneath the body and life of the play.

A limerick has put it succinctly:

> There once was a guy named Othello,
> A dark, disagreeable fellow,
> > After croaking his wife,
> > He took his own life—
> That bird wasn't black, he was yellow! [1]

Let us find a more extended version.

Othello, a general in the service of the Venetian state, has secretly married Desdemona, daughter of the Venetian senator Brabantio. Older than she, Othello has won her love by the romance and fascination of his colorful adventures and rich experience. Haled before the Duke, Othello is accused by Brabantio of carrying off his daughter. Simultaneously comes news of an impending attack against Cyprus by the Turks; and

---

[1] E. M. Robinson, *Piping and Panning* (New York: Harcourt, Brace & Co., 1920). Used by permission of the publishers.

Othello is needed to lead the Venetian forces. Othello explains to the council of state by what simple means he won Desdemona. Brabantio, in the exigencies of war, acquiesces in a situation beyond his control, and reluctantly hands his daughter to the Moor, who sets off to Cyprus leaving her to follow.

Previously, Othello has promoted Cassio, an able young Florentine officer. By this promotion he has offended another officer, Iago, who in envy plots revenge by inciting Othello to jealousy. Iago gets Cassio drunk, brings him to dishonor, and has him demoted from his rank. Then Iago inveigles Desdemona into pleading Cassio's favor with Othello. At the same time he craftily instills in Othello's mind that Desdemona is really concerned not with Cassio's troubles but with Cassio himself, that the troubles are just a convenient shield hiding her covert interest in the younger man. By a trick he arranges that a handkerchief given by Othello to Desdemona is passed on to Cassio. Then, by crafty word Iago adds one suggestion to another, until from conduct perfectly innocent, from trifle and coincidence, he weaves a pattern of misconduct which so kindles the deluded husband's undisciplined temper that, as last, in a frenzy of jealous rage, Othello smothers Desdemona in her bed.

He has scarcely done his dreadful deed—so narrow is the margin by which folly brings disaster—when Cassio (whom Iago sent a rough soldier, Roderigo, to assassinate) is brought in wounded. Iago has already killed Roderigo to prevent discovery of the plot, but in Roderigo's pocket are found letters revealing the guilt of Iago and the innocence of Cassio. Iago adds another crime by killing his wife to silence her; but in the general revelation his own part is made clear, and he is led away to judgment and torture. Othello, thunderstruck by the consequences of his senseless jealousy, kills himself with his own sword.

OTHELLO: *The Tragedy of Jealousy*

No other play in Shakespeare, it seems to me, awakens so vividly and painfully the feeling of needless tragedy. And the power in *Othello* is not limited to the stage. No one, I think, can read it through attentively without being gripped to the heart. I have read it in a quiet room alone, and when I have finished, the play has taken hold of my imagination and emotion as powerfully as if I had heard the actors speak and seen the curtain drop. And the phrase that in the silence repeated itself to my mind was the phrase of Othello himself: "The pity of it . . . ! O . . . the pity of it!"

The sense of tragedy in the play is intensified, the somber darkness is deepened, the lurid lights are made more hellish, the ugliness is made more loathsome, by the contrast with Desdemona, the most lovely of Shakespeare's creations as Iago is the most malignant.

From the time Desdemona, a new-made bride who has "felt no age and known no sorrow," walks on the stage to bespeak her devotion to her husband, to the time she is strangled to death, every subtle suggestion that can be brought into play by the greatest literary genius of the ages in the full maturity of his powers, lines and tints her grace and beauty, her goodness and purity, the sureness of her fidelity, the infinite promise of her love.

"I cannot understand it," said Mark Twain to the beautiful Olivia who became his wife. "You are so beautiful; and yet you are as kind, as good, as sweet, as unselfish, as truthful, as sensible, as intelligent as the homeliest woman I ever saw." There are other suggestions concerning women which echo the line of doggerel that "if they're good, they're not good looking; if good-looking they're not good." But if there is one note of harmony in all the discord of the play, it is the spontaneous acknowledgment by all who knew her of the loveliness and goodness of Desdemona.

Her father describes her as:

> A maiden never bold;
> Of spirit so still and quiet that her motion
> Blush'd at herself.

Even Iago, though he ruthlessly plots to "turn her virtue into pitch," calls her a most exquisite lady and pays her one of the finest tributes in all literature. He declares to Cassio that she is "of so free, so kind, so apt, so blessed a disposition, she holds it a vice in her goodness not to do more than she is requested." Cassio himself, that connoisseur of women, calls her "a most fresh and delicate creature," who "is indeed perfection," "and yet withal modest," who "paragons description." The woman who was her companion cries out that Desdemona was "the sweetest innocent that e're did lift up eye." Roderigo, coarse and stupid poltroon with no appreciation of Desdemona's excellence, yet is awed by her beauty and is exploited by Iago all through the play by the tantalizing prospect that possession of her body would be the reward of his dastardliness. And Othello in every word repeats that "the world hath not a sweeter creature." "I do but say what she is: so delicate with her needle; an admirable musician: O, she will sing the savageness out of a bear: of so high and plenteous wit and invention." Even when calling her vilest names, he says:

> O thou weed,
> Who art so lovely fair and smell'st so sweet
> That the sense aches at thee.

When in agony of madness he kisses her, he exclaims:

> Ah, balmy breath, that dost almost persuade
> Justice to break her sword!

He chokes her because he will not

> scar that whiter skin of hers than snow
> And smooth as monumental alabaster.

And he fears that in the act of strangling her, her body and beauty will "unprovide his mind." He kills her as a sacrifice but says after he does it:

> Had she been true,
> If heaven would make me such another world
> Of one entire and perfect chrysolite,
> I'ld not have sold her for it.

Suggestion is piled on suggestion to portray the beauty, the devotion, the friendliness, the incomparable charm, of the "divine Desdemona."

Those who read mystery stories (and probably most of us do; it is our vicarious opportunity of getting away with murder) will be familiar with a particular literary device. The person murdered is often so obnoxious that the murder creates no shock and awakens no sympathy. Shakespeare, by a contrary device, plays on every chord to make the murder more pathetic. It is sufficiently moving that this should happen to any wife who craved her husband's love and roused his hate and stood up at the last with that poignant cry: "I know not how I lost him." But that it should happen to a creature so fair and lovely, so virtuous and innocent, does all the more, as the dramatist knew full well, call forth that poignant cry: "The pity of it . . . ! O . . . the pity of it!"

Shakespeare accentuates the poignancy of his picture by his creation of Othello. Othello also is the center not of anger but of sympathy. When we meet him, he is a brave, capable soldier. He has already won distinction in combat and come to the maturity of his years—gallant and magnanimous in spirit, a man of simple mind and large heart. He is ruined by jealousy, but he would not be ruined save that he was duped and goaded by one infinitely cleverer than himself. Even then, he cannot be ruined by his vices. He is ruined only by his virtues.

Othello, as Shakespeare takes pains to show, was not jealous by nature. He himself says at the end that he was not easily made jealous, "but, being wrought," was "perplexed in the extreme." At first he puts Iago's insinuations in their proper place:

> Think'st thou I'ld make a life of jealousy,
> To follow still the changes of the moon
> With fresh suspicions?
> . . . .
> 'Tis not to make me jealous
> To say my wife is fair, feeds well, loves company,
> Is free of speech, sings, plays and dances well;
> Where virtue is, these are more virtuous.

He speaks with a proper pride in Desdemona's charm, with confidence in her fidelity. As long as jealousy is not present, everything is in its proper proportion and trifles are left to be trifles. But as soon as jealousy enters, all the proportions begin to change. Trifles light as air now loom up with sinister suggestion. Othello might have said with Iago: "My jealousy shapes faults that are not." He begins to think that as Desdemona deceived her father by concealing her marriage, so now, perhaps, she deceives him. Then it is but a short step to thinking that all she does is false. Soon, "farewell the tranquil mind! farewell content!" Emilia wisely says:

> Jealous souls will not be answer'd so;
> They are not ever jealous for the cause,
> But jealous for they are jealous: 'tis a monster
> Begot upon itself, born on itself.

Othello begins to doubt himself. At first he had been confident. He said, "She had eyes and chose me." Life does not change, and then, as now, the hunter was often the hunted.

"I know," says Boreham in one of his essays, "how a woman catches a man. This afternoon I saw it happen. Every time he turns in her direction, he finds her looking at him." Every time Othello spoke to others, he found Desdemona listening to him. Gently she beguiled him into talking to her of his life's experience, so much outranging her shielded years. As Othello said, "She gave me for my pains a world of sighs." (Evidently the bobby soxers are not original when they swoon for current movie idols.) Then, "she wish'd that heaven had made her such a man." When that did not succeed, she cast the fly again.

> And bade me, if I had a friend that loved her,
> I should but teach him how to tell my story,
> And that would woo her.

In brief, she said like Longfellow's heroine, "Why don't you speak for yourself, John?"

> Upon this hint I spake:
> She loved me for the dangers I had pass'd,
> And I loved her that she did pity them.

He wonders now if that were enough. It begins to seem strange even to him that this radiant and beautiful creature has chosen him, a rough soldier of middle age with little in him to charm and with the heavy physical barrier, not only of years, but also of color (though we must remember that the barrier of color would not be nearly so important in the setting of the play as it would be in twentieth-century America). He sees about her men of her own age, men of charm like Cassio, handsome, young, "framed to make women false," and with "all those requisites in him that folly and green minds look after." He thinks of Cassio, who has a way with women, who blithely kisses Iago's wife in Iago's presence, who holds Desdemona's hand as though he has forgotten it is in his, who carries on an affair with Bianca of the street. He watches Cassio now hanging around Desdemona. He discovers that Cassio has Desdemona's handkerchief, and he hears Desdemona persistently pleading favor for Cassio.

Jealousy is the magnifier of trifles. Everything now serves to distort the picture. Once Iago has set the pattern, once he has begun to interpret action with jealous meaning, then with cunning malignancy he warps and changes until finally he makes the most casual meeting take on the most vicious significance, and the most commendable sympathy appear the basest scheming.

Finally, Othello, who has been so magnificent in discipline, whose nature "passion could not shake," loses self-control, becomes so distraught with passion that in the presence of his friends he falls prostrate into fits. He is goaded into such ungovernable fury against Desdemona that he hurls at her disgusting accusations, calls her filthy names, believes her guilty of foulest deeds, strikes her, and, at last, strangles her in her bed. Desdemona dead is not more brought to ruin than Othello still alive. For him too the watcher says: "The pity of it . . . ! O . . . the pity of it!"

To be sure, we run into some academic minds, more interested in theories than in their relation to fact, who think that it would not be quite ladylike for Desdemona to marry a man whose body was black, and who therefore set about toning down the darkness. They cannot have been more horrified than Desdemona's father, who, when he learned that his daughter loved

Othello, thought that only witchcraft could have caused nature so preposterously to err. It is obvious that if Desdemona had merely married someone who happened to be a shade more brunette than herself, she would not have taken an action in which she would need to defy all the ladies of Venice; and, indeed, such an interpretation would steal from the play much of its dramatic strength. The plain theatergoer, who takes Othello at his own repeated descriptions as black, has more insight than the critics with their attenuated and unconvincing explanations that he was merely a stylish beige.

We have also the theorists who would explain that jealousy is not the emotion of the play. It is true that all Shakespeare's tragedies are too subtle to be described by one abstract noun. When we say that *Hamlet* is the tragedy of indecision or *Othello* the tragedy of jealousy, we are using a brevity to make a title. That is simple and clear to all. The trouble comes only when we run into doctrinaire minds with their pontifical dogmatism that Hamlet's trouble is not indecision and Othello's is not jealousy. They cannot understand that when they are through, Shakespeare is dead and his plays museum pieces. Yet they have had distinguished company, usually critics who deal more in ideas than in drama. Samuel Taylor Coleridge, for example, is representative of those who declare that Othello is moved by honor, not by jealousy. Others say that Othello was governed by the tenet of the Moslem faith which says that the unfaithful wife must die. Still others, far too naïve in their reading of human nature, declare that Othello is guilty only of judicial murder, that he felt Desdemona had wronged him and might wrong others, and therefore wished to save the world from her evil.

The listener in the audience who is caught up in the passion of the play will not be greatly bothered with these follies of the academic mind. Listen to Othello in a passion wanting to tear Desdemona to pieces. He is not then entirely judicial. True,

43

Othello kills Desdemona as a sacrifice. He convinces himself that he is not jealous but is merely the embodiment of eternal justice. In like manner Torquemada, who gave his victims to the torture of the Inquisition, did it for the good of the church and the glory of God. "Whenever a man does a thoroughly stupid thing," says Oscar Wilde, "it is always from the noblest motives."

The rationalizations which Othello made to himself are quite unworthy. The rationalizations which others have made to the world are too weak to be convincing. The elementary passion of the play is jealousy, jealousy as cruel as the grave, jealousy which brought a noble soul to ruin and spread disaster all around him.

The excellencies of Desdemona and Othello are countered in the play by the malignant villainy of Iago. As Othello is guilty of jealousy, Iago is guilty of envy. The two are not the same. Jealousy is a distortion of love, envy a suppuration of hate. Jealousy springs from the sense of wrong at being robbed of a precious thing owned by right and justice; envy springs from covetousness of someone else's good. Jealousy, though it "work like madness in the brain," may have elements of greatness; envy is the signature of a mean soul.

The tragedy of Othello's jealousy was a contingent tragedy of Iago's envy. Iago envied the love of Desdemona gained by the rough, elder soldier; he envied the personal success attained by the rival with the black skin; he envied the quality of life and character which rebuked his envy. He said of Othello:

> He hath a daily beauty in his life
> That makes me ugly.

Iago knew only one way to rise superior to Othello, and indeed to all others about him, and that was not to elevate himself but to debase them. He found a vicious joy in the pain and calamity of others, because his was the mind which outwitted them, his the hand which struck them down. In all literature Iago is probably the premier of villains. Fagin may be more detestable in his petty meanness, Richard the Third more completely the inhuman spirit sold to the devil, Satan, as Milton pictured him, loftier and more magnificent; but none of them more subtly than Iago the incarnation of human iniquity.

We must remember, of course, that only a poor actor plays Iago so that he seems a villain. The characteristic villain of the stage has villainy written all over him. As soon as he crosses the door with his slick hair and his sidelong glances, his waxed mustache and his evil leer, a cautious housewife, says a modern writer, would begin counting her spoons or reaching for a hatpin. But villainy is not written upon Iago. Virtue is written upon him. One word follows him everywhere he goes, "Honest." "Honest Iago," is repeated constantly. Desdemona and Othello alike believe in his honesty. Iago is not even of flattering speech like Cassio; he is just a plain, blunt man, kind and true. This is what makes him such a "viper and hellish villain."

The essence of his villainy is that it is entirely unsuspected. Nobody knows him for what he is save only Roderigo. To Roderigo, Iago reveals himself with amazing frankness. Why he should do so to such a lout is hard to understand, unless it be in some deep need of personality, felt by saint and villain, for some person to whom one can speak with freedom, some person in the presence of whom one can let the churning current of one's inner thought overflow the dam. From Roderigo we learn about Iago. Even there we face a dilemma. Iago is such an inveterate liar that he may be lying even when he purports to reveal himself. To guard against that, Shakespeare supports Iago's revelations to Roderigo by Iago's soliloquies. In the soliloquies we hear what Iago says to himself; we see what goes on in the chambers of his imagery.

We like to think that all evil men are unattractive, cowardly, and false. Iago shows our error. He is a brave, poised, polished gentleman. He never loses his nerve, he never flinches, he never fails. We are reminded of a painting of the devil in a city of Europe. At first glance the subtle resemblance to Christ deceives one completely. So it is with Iago. No man, it has been said, was ever as great as Sir Wilfred Laurier looked. No man was ever as open and honest as Iago looked; and yet he belonged to the company of "men slugs and human serpentry."

We note this characteristic. Like Richard the Third, Iago suspected villainy in everyone else. He suspected Othello. He suspected his own wife. He suspected Cassio. He suspected Roderigo, and he was confident that even Desdemona could be tempted into vice. He suspected everybody, and, wherever he went, he sowed suspicion and distrust.

Iago planted and nurtured the jealousy that came to evil bloom in Othello's heart. Well might the bewildered general in his tragedy look down at Iago's feet and, not seeing them different from others, believe it a fable that credits the devil with cloven hoofs.

These three—Desdemona, Othello, and Iago—and the interplay of their lives create the tragedy of the play. Swinburne says: "Were there no other proof . . . of the palpable truth that Shakespeare excelled all other men of all time . . . as a creator of man and woman, there would be overflowing and overwhelming proof of it in the characters and interaction of these three characters." [2]

[2] A. C. Swinburne, *Three Plays of Shakespeare* (New York: Harper & Bros., 1909), p. 41.

Yet Shakespeare shows that of the three, Iago has his way. Othello, gallant, simple, with the kind of greatness that might have given Desdemona the love and happiness she craved, is exploited, duped, ruined, done to death. Desdemona, beautiful, gifted, loyal, made for love and husband and home, is maligned, rejected, murdered. Iago has his way. It is true that he is sentenced to judgment and torture, but not till he has ruined those whom his evil hate has encompassed. There is no happy end. There is no last-minute chance. There is no poetic justice. The curtain falls on the wreckage of happiness, on the ruin of beautiful and noble lives, on the triumph of malignancy, on the victory of evil. It leaves us awed with the mystery of life and baffled by the bitter release of death.

What then of the moral meaning of a play in which life so ends? We cannot put it better than it was put by George Morrison:

Let the answer to that be given by the reader.

Where do his sympathies lie? Does he crown Iago as a victor? Does he not deeply feel that Iago (apart from any torture that may await him) is ruined, lost, and damned, an outcast from the light, unclean, a living death?

And with equal intensity does he not feel, even to the point of tears, that it were ten thousand times better to be Desdemona in her gentleness, ten thousand times better to be Othello, for all his sin and suicide, than the vile wretch whose evil slew them?

This is the moral power of Shakespeare. He never twists the facts. But he leaves you, in the midst of hideous facts, loathing the evil, cleaving with all your being to what is high and true and good, spite of its sin and failure, and so aligning yourself, perhaps unconsciously, with the Eternal, who reigns, though clouds and darkness are around His throne.[3]

---

[3] *Op. cit.*, p. 118.

[4]

MACBETH
The Tragedy of Ambition

OF THE four tragedies which we study in these chapters only one can be said to be in the modern temper. This one is *Othello*. In *Othello* there are no witches, no ghosts, no supernatural portents, no impossible reappearance of characters in thin disguise. Othello happens to be a general and happens to be in Venice and Cyprus, but these details are incidental. For the essentials he might just as fittingly be the manager of a business office in New York or Toronto. *Othello* is timeless.

Macbeth is a period piece. It brings us back to the medieval mind and sets the play in medieval cast. It is laid in the environs of the supernatural, in an atmosphere where

> Light thickens, and the crow
> Makes wing to the rooky wood.

It is haunted by wild and direful shapes. It makes us see sights not shown to mortal eyes and hear unearthly music. It faces us with things that cannot be. Yet, such is the greatness of the dramatist, we lose no sense of reality; and even in the midst of unfamiliar modes of thought we know that we are dealing with changeless and timeless sins and passions.

Let us, then, turn to the story. It is the best of all Shakespeare's murder stories. And, as usual, it is not a story original with Shakespeare. It is an old story founded on fact. It is told by George Buchanan in his *Latin History of Scotland* and also by Holinshed in the *Chronicles* (first published in 1577), which were Shakespeare's chief rustling ground. Once more the poetic and dramatic genius of Shakespeare transformed a common and sordid story into the essentials of pity and terror.

According to the story, Macbeth and Banquo, generals of Duncan, king of ancient Scotland, are returning victoriously from battle against the rebel Macdonwald. At a wild place upon the heath the generals encounter three witches, who prophesy that Macbeth will be thane (that is, baron) of Cawdor and king of Scotland; and that Banquo will be "lesser than Macbeth, and greater," "not so happy, yet much happier," that he will not be king but will be the father of kings.

While Macbeth and Banquo are still marveling at the strangeness of this announcement so seemingly impossible, a herald arrives to tell them that the thane of Cawdor has been found guilty of treason; and that, as a reward for victory, the king has given the vacant office and title to Macbeth.

These amazing tidings, making true the first of the prophecies, stirs in Macbeth's heart a strange hope that there may be destiny in the second prophecy. He sends a letter telling the exciting news to his wife, a woman as ambitious as her husband and more unscrupulous. She sees with realism that her husband, a victorious and popular general, already thane of Glamis and thane of Cawdor, may very well take the next step to the throne if Duncan should die.

Already in the story we have the feeling of direful events to be. We can understand the apprehension of Simon Tappertit in *Barnaby Rudge:* "Something will come of this. I hope it mayn't be human gore."

Opportunity follows hope. The king pays a special visit to Macbeth's castle to honor him for his victory. He is to remain at the castle but a single night, and Lady Macbeth, realizing that audacity is the necessary ingredient of success, drugs the king's guards and takes their daggers, intending to murder the king as he sleeps. Some chance resemblance of the sleeping king to her father turns her from her purpose, but she goads her husband to the deed from which she herself recoils. Then she returns to the place of murder to smear the sleeping guards with blood.

Morning brings discovery of the murder and a great outcry in the castle. Macbeth in seeming fury kills instantly the two bemused and bloodstained guards, and thus effectively silences any defense they might make. Despite the well-acted grief of Macbeth and his wife, all does not seem right to the rest of the visitors.

> For murder, though it have no tongue, will speak
> With most miraculous organ.
>> *Hamlet,* Act II, scene 2

Duncan's two sons, Malcolm and Donalbain, at the castle with their father, suspect the truth and flee to England for their own safety.

Macbeth assumes the crown but soon finds that he has made an uneasy conquest. Everyone who reads murder stories of the present day is familiar with the pattern in which the first murder makes necessary a second murder to fulfill the purpose of the first, and the second murder then calls for a third murder. So in breathless sequence the novel decorates the path of its devious progress with a direful succession of expendable corpses.

Macbeth discovers a similar compulsion. He begins to think of the witches' prophecy that Banquo's sons will be kings. He be-

gins to fear that he has grasped but a barren scepter, that all
his hazards will end only in giving the throne to Banquo's line.
As he has committed the first murder to fulfill the first prophecy,
now he plans another to frustrate the second prophecy. He in-
vites Banquo to a great feast, but hires murderers to kill him
and Fleance, his son, while they are out riding before the banquet. The murderers fumble. Banquo is killed, but his son
escapes.

At the dinner—to which the guest of honor does not arrive
—though all the others see nothing, Macbeth sees Banquo's
ghost filling the one empty chair. He is so terrified that, like
the king during the play in *Hamlet,* he unmistakably betrays
his guilty secret.

In his terror he seeks again the three witches to ask them
what the future holds. The witches warn him to beware of
Macduff but incite him to be "bloody, bold and resolute," and
equivocally tell him that he can never be vanquished till Birnam
Wood shall march against him; and that his charmed life may
never be harmed by any "of woman born."

Equivocal prophecy is as ancient as time. A famous oracle
once gave the word to an emperor, "Thou shalt go thou shalt
return never in battle shalt thou perish," but left out the
punctuation which determines the meaning of the sentence.
Another oracle told King Croesus that if he marched against
Cyprus, he would destroy a great empire, but omitted to say
which empire. The Parsee in *Moby Dick* told mad Captain
Ahab that he would never be drowned till he saw two coffins
upon the Pacific, but did not add that ships might be coffins.
People have always heard some voice urging them to go the
way they want to go.

Macbeth hears what he wants, and thinks that once more he
can sleep in spite of thunder. When he returns from the witches,
he learns that Macduff, against whom the witches have warned

him, has fled to England to aid Malcolm, the murdered Duncan's son. In a rage he seizes the castle of Macduff and has Lady Macduff and her children murdered and with them even their most distant relations.

Thus murder has led to murder; and Macbeth could now say like Milton's Satan, "Only in destroying do I find ease to my relentless thought."

This last bloody deed alienates all his chief supporters. Those who can, flee to England to join Macduff. The rest, who, like the queen's doctor, "think but dare not speak," pray success to the English armies.

The desperate monarch, beloved and honored so short a time before, begins to feel that the throne is a lonely place. He sits there like an Ishmael, with every man's hand against him. His loneliness is made worse when Lady Macbeth, the sharer of his secrets and the partner of his crimes, loses her reason and dies.

Left all alone, trusting no one, the forsaken king, filled with the madness of a false confidence in the witches' prophecies, waits in his castle for the approach of Macduff's army.

As the siege begins, Malcolm, in an early use of camouflage, orders each soldier to cut a branch off a tree and hold it before him. A superstitious watchman rushes in to Macbeth to say that Birnam Wood is moving toward the castle. "Liar and slave!" shouts Macbeth, as fear that the very universe is against him strikes into his heart.

In desperate reliance on the one remaining prophecy, that he can be harmed by none "of woman born," Macbeth now leads a foolish sortie against the approaching army from behind the safety of his castle walls. When he meets Macduff himself upon the field, he hurls against his enemy the mad boast of invincibility. Macduff replies tauntingly that he was not born but was "from his mother's womb untimely ripped" (the description, of course, for what we now call a Caesarean operation). Utterly betrayed, Macbeth, with a curse upon the witches' deceitful words, rushes to his last fight and is killed and then beheaded.

By the time we have watched these grim events, we have supped full of horror. As in *King Lear,* Shakespeare accentuates the feeling of tragedy by shadow and gloom and the terror of storm and thunder. In *Macbeth,* however, he uses, to a degree matched nowhere else, the dramatic effect of darkness. The vision of the dagger, the murder of Duncan, the murder of Banquo, the sleepwalking of Lady Macbeth, all come at night. Macbeth visits the witches in the smoky cavern and there converses with "black and midnight hags." Almost all scenes are placed either at night or in some dark spot. In the whole drama we see the wholesome light of outdoors only twice: first, when Banquo sees the Martins flitting around the castle of death; and second, when the avenging army gathers to rid the earth of its shame.

The darkness is always broken by eerie light. The faces are lighted for us by torches and candles, and the flickering gleams shine constantly upon one color, the color of blood. After the disappearance of the witches into the "fog and filthy air," a bleeding soldier is the cause of the first spoken word in the action of the play, "What bloody man is that?" Before Macbeth himself makes his first appearance, he is described "with his brandish'd steel, which smoked with bloody execution" as he smote his enemy and "unseam'd him from the nave to the chaps, and fixed his head upon our battlements." The murderer appears in the banquet room with blood rubbed upon his face. Banquo himself has twenty gashes on his head. Macbeth gazes at his hands so dyed with blood that the whole ocean cannot wash them clean, and Lady Macbeth puts her hands away from her face to escape the smell of blood and says, concerning Duncan, "Who would have thought the old man to have had so much blood in him?"

Through all the play there is extraordinary dramatic exploitation of darkness and blood and flickering gleams from candles and torches.

Macbeth is in some respects the forerunner of the horror story of today. It makes *Frankenstein* seem a tale for the more elderly readers of a supermarket magazine.

In this gloom Shakespeare pursues the study of a great soul brought to ruin by unprincipled ambition. Like Othello, Macbeth is introduced to us as a good and honorable person. He is a competent, loyal soldier. He deserves well of his country and is anxious to serve it well. He is a devoted husband, a man of eager ambition, of prodigal energy, and of great courage. But with strong ambition he has but little discipline. He is caught between conflicting urges, with no standards of value to subordinate one to the other. He possesses fine individual qualities regulated by no fixed principles. Shakespeare lets us see that a man reaps the consequences of that one defect, till all his virtues "take corruption from that particular fault" (*Hamlet*, Act I, scene 4) .

The temptations at first are brought to Macbeth from outside. The play begins with the suggestions of the witches. Witches may seem as ridiculous on the modern stage as the fairies of Aeschylus: but we must remember that in Shakespeare's time witches were accepted as real beings. They were not the symbolic presentation of Macbeth's own desires. No one but a modern psychologist would have thought of that. They were not even fates or furies or supernatural beings; they were evil women who had trafficked with the devil, and who possessed weird power and supernatural knowledge. Let us not be too supercilious in judging the audience of Shakespeare's day. Perhaps as we do, we shall cross our fingers, or touch wood, to save ourselves from unhappy consequence.

The witches, then, show the first temptation coming to Macbeth from outside. The witches prophesy, when it seems impossible, that Macbeth will be thane of Cawdor. The witches pass on the suggestion that he will be king. The witches stir restless ambitions within his mind. At the start the play tells us that life can be shaped in part by pressures from without.

Even beyond the witches the compulsion that leads to the murder comes from outside Macbeth's own will. He would never have summoned the resolution to murder his sleeping guest save for the ruthless will of his ambitious wife.

Lady Macbeth herself is one of the most challenging and baffling characters Shakespeare created. She remains the power behind the throne, but we see her only at a distance. In contrast to the care Shakespeare takes to portray, for example, the sensuous charm of Cleopatra and the bewitching loveliness of Desdemona, he has no suggestion whether Lady Macbeth is beautiful and charming or merely a painted battle-ax. The play tells us very little about her. She has been fancied by one as small and fair, blue-eyed and fragile; by another as beautiful and delicate, unoppressed by weight of flesh; by still another as lean, slight, and hard. But all who so picture her must know what Shakespeare does not tell. He says almost nothing about her. A suggestion of frailty appears in her reference to "this little hand," but this is her own description. Her lady in waiting has a different suggestion. She is impressed, even in her mistress' madness, with her dignity of figure. We do know that Lady Macbeth not only manages to marry a general but also manages to keep him in love with her afterward, a task sometimes difficult with men less demanding than generals.

We also know that Lady Macbeth is not, as a hasty reading might hint, simply a cold, heartless woman. Malcolm at the end speaks of "this dead butcher and his fiend-like queen." But this is understandable. He is the son of a murdered father. We see more objectively. She is a woman of great audacity, tremendously strong-willed. Her husband says to her:

> Bring forth men-children only;
> For thy undaunted mettle should compose
> Nothing but males.

She is a woman of ambition, a woman who can coldly make up her mind what she wants and just as coldly make up her mind that she will pay the price, whatever it is, to get what she wants. She is sister under the skin to the modern young woman who said, "When I want something I must have it; I just can't be bothered resisting temptation."

But, as the course of the play makes clear, she is not devoid of womanly instincts; she only conquers them. She fights against the grain. In her iniquity she, like her husband, is stemming a strong tide of better feelings. She has to pray to evil spirits to unsex her, to come to her woman's breasts and take her milk for gall. She has to get herself half drunk before she can overcome the scruples of her conscience (that touch is modern enough). Even then, the vague suggestion that the sleeping victim resembles her father is sufficient to unfix her purpose. And though at last she goads her husband to the deed, even then, as she had not the strength for its performance, so she has not the fortitude to bear its memory. Remorse comes in like a flood. She begins to feel the terror of the dark. Her sleep is broken by horrid dreams, and, like Pilate, she goes through the motion of washing her hands. She gives orders that the light in her room must never go out. As the physician and her lady listen, they hear her tortured speech: "Out damned spot! out, I say! . . . Will these hands ne'er be clean? . . . Here's the smell of blood still: all the perfumes of Arabia will not sweeten this little hand. . . . I tell you yet again, Banquo's buried; he cannot come out on's grave. . . . What's done cannot be undone."

Such a woman is not simply cold and unfeeling. Lady Macbeth is no monster such as Irma Krahmer of Belson, who with equal composure selected her prisoners, some to be her lovers and some to be killed that their skins might make her lampshades. Lady Macbeth is, rather, a woman with one calamitous weakness, a weakness which reveals a strange contrast to her husband. She is defective in imagination. Macbeth has not only the boldness of the soldier; he has also the imagination of a poet. He has the invaluable capacity to see in advance what the deed will look like in retrospect. His wife lacks this reflective power. She feels intensely. Her emotions are a resistless torrent. But she cannot see imaginatively. When she wants to do something, she will do it. She has no idea what it will mean to her afterward. With strangely unjustified confidence in her own cold-bloodedness, she thinks that she will do murder ruthlessly and dismiss it with a sneer. She fancies that a little water will wash away the stain. She does not comprehend the intangibles of such an action. She has no foreknowledge that the deed, when done, will darken her days and fill her life with regret and agony and ceaseless remorse. If she *had been* heartless, she might have done her deed and escaped her agony. She is not heartless, but in her passionate desire to get what she wants, she loses all the proportions of the moral law.

Beyond peradventure it is Lady Macbeth who throws into the scale that balance of will which does the evil deed. Macbeth, for all his ambition, is balanced by a troubled sense of duty, a feeling of loyalty, a triple bond to the king as kinsman, subject, and host. As his wife knows, his nature is "too full o' the milk of human kindness" to be the same in act and valor as in desire. He can "screw his courage to the sticking-place" only when she is able to pour her spirit in his ear. In part, then, the forces that wreak Macbeth's ruin are brought upon him from outside.

Nevertheless, the play also shows us clearly that the tragedy of Macbeth is not in the final analysis imposed from without. Macbeth himself nowhere shifts the burden to anyone else. The defect in character to which the deed must be ascribed is the defect in himself. When he sees the dagger gleaming before him in the darkness, he says: "Thou marshall'st me the way that I was going." And he could say the same to the witches and to his wife. They persuade him to do what he wants to do.

Why is he so excited by the witches' words? Banquo is not moved by what they say. He states bluntly that he neither begged nor feared their favors nor their hate. Malignant spirits were as universal in Macbeth's day as microbes are in ours, and people as readily shuffled off their threat. Macbeth is excited because the witches suddenly give form and definition to greed as yet unpurposed. They add fuel to fires already kindled. They bring an idea to a mind prepared to receive it. Before twenty-four hours have passed, he is saying:

> Stars, hide your fires;
> Let not light see my black and deep desires.

When Lady Macbeth coldly proposes murder, Macbeth is not surprised. He does not reject it. He says evasively, "We will speak further." Shakespeare lets us see that the susceptible disposition meets the tempting opportunity. What life does to you depends upon what life finds in you.

Macbeth's defect, however, is the defect of greatness. Writing to his wife, he says of the witches, "They met me in the day of success." Were he a failure, the witches could not tempt him with their audacious words. But he is a young man going places. He is already a success, and he is greedy of greater success. Any man going ahead is in danger, if he has strong ambition without strong principles. Always there is a temptation not to let moral scruples handicap anything that brings success. Macbeth is evil, not in the ambition, but in the willingness to pay too great a price. He does not know how to put first things first. For tangibles excellent in themselves he sacrifices intangibles wherein all the values of life ultimately reside.

Scarcely has he done his evil deed to crown his great ambition, when he feels that it is not worth the cost. Bitterly he says:

> Had I but died an hour before this chance,
> I had lived a blessed time.

He envies the king whom he has killed.

> Duncan is in his grave;
> After life's fitful fever he sleeps well;
> Nothing,
> Can touch him further.

He feels that it were better to be dead with Duncan than to live with the scorpions of his own conscience.

In time he stands before us a miserable and haggard criminal, finding all of life changed, discovering that now there is no worth or meaning anywhere, and pouring out his misery in words of unutterable despair:

> Out, out, brief candle!
> Life's but a walking shadow, a poor player
> That struts and frets his hour upon the stage

And then is heard no more: it is a tale
Told by an idiot, full of sound and fury,
Signifying nothing.

From the moment he commits his crime he finds not a single interval of human companionship, of warmth or happiness. The gifts which could have made a noble life merely give him everything he has envied, and leave him with nothing he now desires.

At the end he stands a tortured soul, knowing too late that his victories are apples of Sodom already turned to dust and ashes.

One need not question now whether there are spiritual values in Shakespeare. From any pulpit was there ever preached a more powerful sermon on the text: "What shall it profit a man, if he shall gain the whole world, and lose his own soul?"

[5]

KING LEAR
The Tragedy of Ingratitude

THE FOUR tragedies—*Hamlet, Othello, Macbeth,* and *King Lear*—were all written in the first decade of the seventeenth century, between 1600 and 1610, when Shakespeare's genius was burning its brightest and concentrating its flame upon the destiny of man as determined by his inner self. Of the four, *King Lear* is acknowledged as the greatest in certain respects. Swinburne says: "If nothing were left of Shakespeare but the single tragedy of *King Lear,* it would still be plain, as it is now, that he was the greatest man that ever lived." [1]

King Lear is perhaps the least known of the four tragedies and certainly the least popular. *King Lear* conforms to Mark Twain's definition, "A classic is something which everybody wants to have read and nobody wants to read."

King Lear is in one respect strikingly different from the others. In the others good men degenerate; in *King Lear* a bad man is redeemed. Shakespeare introduces Othello and Macbeth, and even Hamlet, as likable and admirable men. One student told me some time ago that she thought Othello was just perfect. Shakespeare was too wise to make his characters perfect.

[1] A. C. Swinburne, *op. cit.* (New York: Harper & Bros., 1909), p. 16.

Yet, certainly, he introduced Othello and Macbeth as men of magnificent qualities.

In contrast Shakespeare introduces Lear as thoroughly un-likable—a stupid, arbitrary, bad-tempered old man. We begin with no liking for him whatever. But in time we see him as "a man more sinn'd against than sinning." At the end our hearts are filled with an overflowing pity.

As usual the story is not original. In early legend Lear was an old British sea god. Through the centuries the tale reappeared in many versions. It is the kind familiar in all folklore. It is a variation of the Cinderella theme. A play of the same title, though differently spelled, was being given in London while Shakespeare was writing his version. But, as Landor says, Shakespeare is more original than the original because he breathed upon the dead bodies and brought them to life.

Let us, then, begin with the story. Lear, king of ancient Britain, has three daughters—Goneril, wife of the duke of Al-bany; Regan, wife of the duke of Cornwall; and Cordelia, for whose hand the duke of Burgundy and the king of France are suitors. Intending to relinquish the burdens of state, the old king plans to divide his kingdom, like Gaul, in three parts, and give it to his three daughters. Before he announces the division, the vain and self-willed old man bids them tell which loves him most. Disraeli once said, "Everyone likes flattery and when you come to royalty you must lay it on with a trowel." [2] The daugh-ters of Lear thought of it before Disraeli. They knew that their old father's idea of an agreeable person was a person who agreed with him. Goneril, the eldest, declares that she loves her father more than words can tell, that he is dearer to her than the light of her own eye. She adds a good deal of similar stuff easy

[2] G. W. E. Russell, *Collections & Recollections* (London: Thos. Nelson & Sons), p. 221.

to counterfeit when there is no real affection. The king, in modern phrase, laps it up and bestows on her and her husband, the duke of Albany, one third of the kingdom.

Regan, the second daughter, outflatters Goneril. Regan declares that all her sister has said is inadequate to express her own feelings. She finds all other joys dead in comparison with the love she has for her dear father. Lear then bestows on Regan and her husband, the duke of Cornwall, another third of his kingdom.

Now Shakespeare introduces his heroine, Cordelia, one of the loveliest women in his gallery. He takes no pains to invest her with the beauty and fascination of Desdemona, who would have been an event just walking across a hotel lobby. Cordelia has, rather, the attractiveness of quiet charm and resolute character:

> Her voice was ever soft,
> Gentle and low, an excellent thing in woman.

Her faithfulness, courage, and character place her among the immortals. It is strange how Shakespeare can create so clear an impression with so few strokes of his pen. We do not see Cordelia at length as we see Desdemona, Cleopatra, and Imogen. Cordelia appears only in four out of twenty-six scenes and speaks little more than one hundred lines. But the master has interpreted her more fully with a few strokes than lesser artists could do with a full portrait.

When her father speaks to her, Cordelia is utterly disgusted by her sisters' insincerity. She is of different metal. She has not the "glib and oily art, to speak and purpose not." She cannot heave her heart into her mouth. She tells her father, in restrained contrast to her gushing sisters, that she loves him according to the duty of a daughter, nothing more and nothing less. The petulant old man, spoiled by lifelong servility, is annoyed by the note of realism and cautions Cordelia to mend her speech or he will mar her fortunes. She replies affectionately that her love is richer than her tongue. She loves and honors him, but she cannot say that she will love nobody else. She will not, as her sisters, marry a husband to love only a father.

The old king has been made egregiously vain by the cringing, groveling timeservers surrounding the throne. He is a glowing witness of Lord Acton's dictum that "power tends to corrupt, and absolute power corrupts absolutely." In despotic petulance and childishness he now determines that he will make his daughter sorry. So he disinherits her completely; and, stipulating only that they must care for him as long as he lives, he divides his kingdom between the two daughters who have fawned on him with their flattery.

Upon this the duke of Burgandy, who knows how to trim his sail to the wind, withdraws his suit for Cordelia's hand. But the king of France, then a very tiny little kingdom, is made of better metal. Though Cordelia is penniless and under a cloud, he takes her away as his wife, saying, "She is herself a dowry."

As for Lear's own court, even in the face of such preposterous injustice, none of the obsequious courtiers, save only the earl of Kent, has courage to speak a word to offend the petulant monarch or the coming heiresses of power. Kent stubbornly persists in rebuking the king, until, like a patient who vents his anger upon the doctor, Lear sentences Kent to exile from England.

When we meet Lear, he is not an attractive person. After so much, we are sure that whatever he may get, he will deserve.

A second story is now interwoven with the first. This familiar Shakespearean practice here has one difference. The subordinate story repeats the theme of the main story. Again an old man, the duke of Gloucester, foolish and self-willed, wrongs the child who loves him, meets with monstrous ingratitude from the child he favors, is tortured and at last driven to death.

Gloucester, in the undisciplined days of his youth, had become father to an illegitimate son, Edmund. Edmund has been well cared for by Gloucester but carries a bitter grudge against the legitimate son Edgar. Edmund plots the overthrow of Edgar with a jealous ambition that, as he puts it, "the base shall top the legitimate." He poisons his father's mind against Edgar and callously plots to oust his father, to set aside his legitimate half-brother, and to seize the dukedom for himself. The two plots interweave; and steadily the evil deeds work retribution.

Lear's sufferings are not slow in coming. As soon as his two daughters have power, they drop pretense and show their true colors. They make it plain that they deem his old age a burden, and their professed love changes into the bitterest contempt. A doggerel couplet states it:

> He gives his daughters the estate:
> The daughters then give him the gate.

Quickly Lear learns that the winter wind is not as cold as the heart of a thankless child.

More than once Shakespeare plays with ingratitude. You remember in *Julius Caesar:*

> When the noble Caesar saw him stab,
> Ingratitude, more strong than traitors' arms,
> Quite vanquish'd him: then burst his mighty heart.

Only in *King Lear*, however, does Shakespeare put ingratitude at the center, and come to grips with that "marble-hearted fiend."

The old man's feeble strength is relentlessly sapped by constant and calculated cruelty. Finally, his mind breaks under the strain. One night amid a terrible storm, which rends the heavens with sheets of fire and bursts of horrid thunder, he rushes out on the heath, where he sees nature matching the tumult in his own breast; and in unbalanced frenzy he defies the elements less cruel than his unnatural daughters.

His mad flight into the wilds is but the beginning of his purgatory. A poor, infirm, despised old man, he goes from torment to torment. He wanders helplessly in the wood, unrecognized and unhonored, penniless and witless, hunted by his daughters who now want to get rid of him completely, and saved from bitter death only by the faithful Kent, who, though banished, has returned in disguise to be with his old master in time of need.

The lines of the play now become more complicated. Technically, the interweaving of the two plots is one of the masterpieces of Shakespeare's skill. But it becomes hard for the unfamiliar reader to keep the issues clear. Perhaps many a person's response to *King Lear* is: "I cannot understand it, so it must be great."

The duke of Gloucester, his mind poisoned by his illegitimate son, Edmund, banishes Edgar, his legal son. But Gloucester, though sadly duped, never loses the attributes of a gentleman. He seeks to find and help the hapless Lear. In the tyrannical retaliation of Regan, Gloucester is stripped of his estate and, in perhaps the cruelest act presented on any stage, has his eyes put out by Regan's husband, Cornwall. The blinded Gloucester becomes a second fugitive, also attended by a character in disguise, Edgar, his banished son. (In a Shakespearean play no character in disguise is ever recognized.)

Then, from afar, Cordelia, now queen of France, comes to England as a sort of *dea ex machina* to right the various wrongs.

She brings an army to rescue her father, and a doctor to treat his mind. The doctor succeeds, but the army is defeated; Cordelia and Lear are taken prisoner. Cordelia is hanged by Edmund's order, and Lear dies of a broken heart. But, with a startling touch of drama at the last, Lear, in the very moment of death, is seized by a wayward fancy that Cordelia lives; and he dies in the midst of tragedy with a burst of joy upon his face.

The unjust, however, reap their grim reward. All their success withers in their grasp. Goneril and Regan reach the lowest depths to which woman may fall. Each turns her affections from her husband to the adventurer Edmund, and the rivalry of their illicit love kindles a hate for each other which exceeds their hate for their father. Goneril poisons Regan, and follows that unnatural deed by taking her own life. Goneril and Regan are undoubtedly the worst women Shakespeare ever drew— lecherous, treacherous, pitiless, remorseless. Shakespeare makes us feel that the best of all creatures is a good woman, and that the vilest of all creatures is a wicked woman. His judgment of women is that when they are good, they are very, very good; and when they are bad, they are horrid.

At the conclusion of the play the treachery of Edmund is proved by the faithful Edgar, who in combat mortally wounds his illegitimate brother. After this surfeit of calamity, the duke of Albany, who has had no sympathy with his wife's heartless treatment of her father, takes over the kingdom.

Even this sketchy outline can perhaps suggest something of the vast proportions of the play. It is a dinosaur of a drama. It has been called Shakespeare's greatest creation, but his least actable play. It is difficult to act, because it is on so stupendous a scale. Many of the great Shakespearean actors have disliked playing in *King Lear*. Eugene Field once commented on an actor who played Lear in Boston, "He played the King as though someone had led the ace." A few actors have found in *King Lear* a supreme triumph. Garrick's performance was unforgettable. It is said that when he cried, "Fool, I shall go mad," the whole audience chilled with horror. Edmund Kean's Lear was said to present Shakespeare by flashes of lightning. Yet however great the central figure, the play is filled with improbabilities and inconsistencies, overshadowed with characteristic Shakespearean gloom, and overpacked with emotion. It is a succession of "horrid shapes and shrieks and sights unholy." The total impression is one of almost unendurable horror. Kent himself said, "All's cheerless, dark and deadly," and Albany, that it is a "judgment of the heavens," that "makes us tremble."

The whole story is so overcast in tragedy that for a hundred years after Shakespeare's death the last act was changed to give a happy ending. It was not till 1837 that MacReady returned to the full Shakespearean text. It is not surprising that this should have been so. We commonly seek a happy ending. Normally in literature we get one. However the lines are tangled throughout the tale, at the last evil is banished and virtue rewarded. We are properly delivered from the rack of this tough world.

It is the measure of Shakespeare's greatness that he does not let his plays become a shelter from the cruelty of life. He does not end with wedding bells. He does not play with the convention that life brings poetic justice. He makes us feel how different life would be, could we remold it nearer to our heart's desire.

More than any other play *King Lear* awakens this feeling. There the clouds and darkness seem to shroud the agony of all the world. It is no accident, but a powerful dramatic device, which breaks the pitiless elements upon a poor old man already broken by his pitiless daughters. It is no accident that the tempest-driven world howls around a tempest-driven soul. The storms without picture the storms within—as though all nature were in sympathy with human passions and experience, as though the universe were torn by the sins and struggles of the soul. John Masefield says that Shakespeare has poured into the soul of Lear such misery "that the cracking of the great heart is a thing of joy." No other image in literature, he declares, is "so fierce with imaginative energy." [3] Yet as we watch, we feel how far better than the shallow satisfaction of a cheerful ending it is to see what happens to the soul in great waters.

In *King Lear* (as I pointed out) there is something that is in no other tragedy. In the others souls are lost by sin; in *King Lear* a soul is saved by suffering. The old man who dies is vastly different from the one we meet in the first scene. Then he was vain and arrogant and cruel, warped by irresponsible power. But his terrible suffering quickens his vision, widens his sympathy, and, singularly enough in a Shakespearean play, leads him to penitent prayer.

His suffering in the storm awakens his mind to think of those whom he has forgotten: the homeless and the hungry. Swinburne points out that here we have the first fiery protest against social wrongs ever presented upon the stage; and that Shakespeare brought it forth not from Hamlet, with his infinite capacity for reflection, but from Lear, who had never thought upon the matter until he himself was exposed "to feel what wretches feel." The wrongs done by indifference as well as by cruelty, by negligence as well as by crime, "were hidden from the marvellous wisdom of Hamlet and revealed to the more marvellous insanity of Lear." [4] Swinburne also points out the significance for us that this could be thundered from the English stage at the dawn of the seventeenth century. Even

[3] *William Shakespeare* (London: Thornton Butterworth, 1939), pp. 191, 194.
[4] *Op. cit.*, p. 20.

had there been German or Russian Shakespeares, nothing of the sort could have been whispered or muttered or hinted on the boards of a Russian theater. It could not in Russia today.

George H. Morrison says that nothing is more beautiful in Shakespeare than the purification of the soul of Lear under "the slings and arrows of outrageous fortune" (*Hamlet,* Act III, scene 1). We can agree. To turn from Lear in the first act to Lear in the last act is like turning from a Saul of Tarsus to a Paul the apostle. Listen as Lear speaks to Cordelia:

> Come, let's away to prison:
> We two alone will sing like birds i' the cage:
> When thou dost ask me blessing, I'll kneel down
> And ask of thee forgiveness: so we'll live,
> And pray, and sing, and tell old tales, and laugh
> At gilded butterflies, and hear poor rogues
> Talk of court news; and we'll talk with them too,
> Who loses and who wins, who's in, who's out;
> And take upon 's the mystery of things,
> As if we were God's spies.

When Cordelia is led away, Lear says to her:

> Upon such sacrifices, my Cordelia,
> The gods themselves throw incense.

The transformation of character is not confined to Lear himself. Throughout the third act all the good are growing better through suffering, and all the bad are growing worse through success. This is astonishing in a play of Elizabethan England. In the eyes of the audiences for whom Shakespeare wrote, the great—the kings, the conquerors—were the ones to be envied.

70

In *King Lear* Shakespeare turned admiration upon those characters who through trial and tribulation developed inner integrity, humility of mind, compassion for the poor. "The drama of 'King Lear,'" says Lewis Thurber Guild, "is Gothic in its massiveness, and, like the cathedral architecture . . . its arches and windows point upward."[5]

Moreover, in *King Lear,* as in the other plays, *moral law is the scaffolding of the universe.* In all the plays evil is the source of calamity. In *Romeo and Juliet* it is the hatred of the Capulets and the Montagues; in *Macbeth* it is greed and unbridled ambition; in *Othello* the cold iniquity of Iago; in *King Lear* it is ingratitude. In all, evil is the power that wrecks happiness, mars lives, and paves the way to ruin. True it seems that evildoers for a while appear to thrive. They are not unhappy, and they certainly have the power to spread misery and destruction around them. Yet in the end evil is in itself destructive. The world in which evil appears seems somehow at heart to reject it. In that sense the play takes on prophetic quality.

Moreover, though lives gentle and true may be overwhelmed, faith and goodness still shine in the darkness; and the darkness cannot put them out. A superb piece of dramatic irony comes at the end of *King Lear*. Albany prays for Cordelia, "The gods defend her!" Immediately follows the stage direction, "Enter Lear, with Cordelia dead in his arms." The gods do not defend her. The cup of agony is not set aside. Yet, as in *Macbeth,* we feel that it is better to be Duncan murdered at midnight, "his silver skin laced with his golden blood," than to be his haunted murderer; so in *King Lear* we feel it is better to be Cordelia hanged in prison than Goneril and Regan, though they reign in purple. Right and wrong stand before us, different, not from

---

[5] *The Cosmic Ray in Literature* (Nashville: Cokesbury Press, 1929), p. 155.

mere expediency or preferability, but from an immeasurable span of moral superiority. It is the lesson of Job, of the Prophets, of the Revelation, of the Cross itself. It must have been one of the lessons that Shakespeare learned from the Books of God. In *King Lear,* as in so much of Shakespeare, we can always see above the darkness the sheen of the everlasting light.

[6]

RICHARD THE THIRD
The Tragedy of Bad Intention

THE FOUR tragedies just treated are a fitting unity, and it is well to study them in sequence. But they are not the only plays that move amid the eternities. We shall now deal with four other plays of different character: two histories, a comedy, and a romance—although, of course, *Richard III* and *Julius Caesar* are more than history, the *Merchant of Venice* is more than comedy, and *The Tempest* is more than romance. In all of them we shall find, as in the tragedies, the inexorable working of a universe of moral law.

In the historical plays Shakespeare had of necessity to work within arbitrary limits. He had not to invent and develop, but to isolate and transfer from chronological record as much of the essential stuff of human life as would serve dramatic purpose. When he wrote a historical play, he set before the eyes a historical episode; but he played upon it with lights shining from earth and heaven, until the brightness and the shadows separated and illuminated faces and scenes and proportions lost in the darkness of noon. He took an event in time and made it an event in eternity.

73

Richard III is a play which is, as it were, the final act in a longer play. It rounds out an extraordinary cycle of eight plays which together present in systematic procession and awesome proportion an epoch of English history.

The eight plays begin with *Richard II.* Then, as Richard is deposed by Henry the Fourth, the second and third plays picture the strife-torn England of Henry's reign. The fourth play, *Henry V,* portrays the fleeting glory of Agincourt and Henry's accession to the crown of France. Then follow three plays on Henry the Sixth, moving direfully from calamity in France to more dreadful calamity in England.

The Hundred Years' War, which, just before the opening of the plays, had dazzled England with the victories of Crécy and Poitiers, and which in the reign of Henry the Fifth had revived the brief illusion of national grandeur, dwindled under Henry the Sixth to an ignoble end. The long costly struggle and all the sacrifice in English wealth and English blood ended with no more conquest than a precarious hold on the port of Calais.

As though the war abroad had not been sufficient folly, the kings and nobles of England had hardly been expelled from France before they began to divide England in the worse calamity of civil war. For another thirty years the houses of Lancaster and York, by intrigue and assassination, by petty conflict and pitched battle, ravaged their island home for their own selfish ambitions. The three plays of Henry the Sixth are a record of an England that, in the words of Shakespeare, had "long been mad."

Finally, Richard the Third brought the climax of all this calamity. When Richard was slain on Bosworth Field, the Wars of the Roses came to an end. The victor, the Earl of Richmond, took the throne as Henry the Seventh, first of the Tudor monarchs. He ushered in a century which, despite the five terrible years of Bloody Mary, led in total to the spacious days of Queen Elizabeth—who was still reigning when Shakespeare recalled the macrocosm of history in the microcosm of drama.

The eight plays are an artistic unity. They comprise a single drama with one subject and one end toward which their whole creation moves. They picture sordid evil slowly working its own destruction, relentless moral law limning the destiny of a nation.

The plays, it is true, are unequal in merit. Shakespeare, who wrote the opening *Richard II* and the closing *Richard III*, did only patches of some of the intervening plays. Were the whole series on the level of the two Richard plays, the splendor of the single drama, says Stopford Brooke, "would blind the eyes of the intellect and of the soul of man."

Though the eight plays are a unity, they were not produced ploddingly in chronological order. Scholars still dispute whether Shakespeare wrote *Richard III* before writing *Richard II,* and they do not agree on the historical order of the Henry plays. It matters little. When Shakespeare had completed his pattern with one play on Richard the Second, two plays on Henry the Fourth, one play on Henry the Fifth, three plays on Henry the Sixth, and the concluding play on Richard the Third, he had presented national history on a scale not equaled even in the Greek trilogies. He had created in drama a survey of human life vaster and more varied than has ever been comprised in any one unit elsewhere in the history of literature.

I wonder if, since he finished writing, any company of players ever started at *Richard II* and played the entire series in nightly sequence, so that the spectators could watch the mighty tread of destiny through a century of woe, and follow the relentless march of retribution destroying the destroyers of England's peace.

75

As we survey these plays, the prentice work of the master craftsman of all time, we can see how natural it is that Shakespeare should see the issues of human life in national terms before he saw them in universal terms. From the opening of the seventeenth century he looked through the perspective of the sixteenth century to see in panorama the sweep of the fifteenth century. Then he turned from his parochial pedestal in the little isle "set in the silver sea," to become a citizen of earth surveying the life of man in the setting of time and the proportions of eternity.

Shakespeare was writing at one of the most exciting moments in English history. The hearts of his countrymen were being stirred by nascent pride in their own land. The world and England's place in the world had been changed as by magic. English ships were sailing through unknown seas and unfolding a new world that as yet knew only two rights: the right of discovery and the right of conquest.

When Drake sailed up the Thames after circling the earth or plundering Spanish galleons on the Spanish main or singeing the King of Spain's beard in the ports of Spain itself; and especially when an impromptu navy of English fishing vessels manned by English fishermen swept from the seas the Invincible Armada—then the Englishmen of Shakespeare's day began, as their fathers had never done, to feel their own identity, their own strength, their own destiny. They became kindled with a love of native land which was in time to mark every country of the Western world.

The song of England, muted since the first spring notes of Wycliffe and Chaucer, sounded again in Spenser and in Marlowe and echoed like bells from a high tower over every stage where Shakespeare played. Listen to different plays:

Now all the youth of England are on fire.
> *(Henry V*, Act II, scene 1)

This royal throne of kings, this scepter'd isle,
This earth of majesty, this seat of Mars,
This other Eden, demi-paradise;
This fortress built by Nature for herself
Against infection and the hand of war;
This happy breed of men, this little world,
This precious stone set in the silver sea,
Which serves it in the office of a wall,
Or as a moat defensive to a house,
Against the envy of less happier lands;
This blessed plot, this earth, this realm, this England,
. . . .
This land of such dear souls, this dear dear land.
> (*King Richard II*, Act II, scene 1)

This England never did, nor never shall,
Lie at the proud foot of a conqueror,
But when it first did help to wound itself.
. . . .
Come the three corners of the world in arms,
And we shall shock them. Nought shall make us rue,
If England to itself do rest but true.
> *(King John*, Act V, scene 7)

Heaven take my soul, and England keep my bones!
> *(King John*, Act IV, scene 3)

This new pride in England led Shakespeare to look back and describe the agonizing ordeal of foreign and civil strife through which the country had struggled in past times. The national calamities that England had endured had been a tainted legacy of evil men—kings who were "breakers of their own behests," princes who were "truant in the law," and a mindless multitude as savage and ill-disciplined as their rulers.

77

It was as if in an era of peace—if such an era is to follow our time—some dramatist of the twenty-first century should look back to portray the folly and sin, and misery and sorrow, of the long-drawn period between Edward the Peacemaker and Elizabeth the Second. As Milton was to see "a noble and puissant nation rousing herself like a strong man after sleep, and shaking her invincible locks," so Shakespeare saw an England, preserved through bitter trial and purged from awful guilt, gathering her recovered strength and marching proudly through the gateway of a better day.

The episodes of history which are the material of the final play can be briefly and succinctly stated. *Henry VI,* Part III, shows Richard, duke of Gloucester, with characteristic ruthlessness, stabbing to death the captured and defenseless king, and thereby bringing to the throne the incompetent Edward the Fourth.

The final play, *Richard III,* shows Richard, first as duke of Gloucester and later as king, systematically liquidating every person who can possibly threaten his crown or who dares to question his will. Edward the Fourth, indeed, saves himself from Richard's cruelty by quickly dying a natural death. But Richard's other victims include not only the puppets which he uses and casts aside—Earl Rivers, Lord Grey, Lord Hastings, and Sir Thomas Vaughan—but also his own brother Clarence; his first wife, Anne; and his nephews, the two little princes whom his minions smother in the tower. When necessary, Richard delegates assassination; but whenever possible, he kills by his own hand for sheer delight in killing.

Richard's deeds bring their natural consequence in savage hatreds which raise an army against him and, at Bosworth Field, bring to an end his brief and terrible power. His conqueror, the Earl of Richmond (who becomes Henry the Seventh), by his marriage with Elizabeth daughter of Edward the Fourth, unites the two families of Lancaster and York and stops the Wars of the Roses. The end of Richard is the end of an epoch.

Richard III has many foretokens of a theme that reappears in *Julius Caesar* and again in *Macbeth:* a ruthless monarch captures a throne by destroying all who stand in his way; and is himself destroyed by the inexorable consequence of the same evil deeds which have raised him to power.

Richard III, however, is different from the other plays in two particulars. First, it has only one important character. Richard himself dominates the entire play. From the opening scene to the end, where he is conquered by Richmond, no one else is of sufficient consequence to be more than his puppet or his victim. Lady Margaret, who in point of fact has no historical warrant for her appearance, is the only one strong enough to face Richard without fear. She incarnates all the hatred and bitterness that has been conceived and nurtured in the hellish process of civil strife. But she does not affect the movement of the play. She merely stands outside looking at it—an avenging fury hurling bitter curses, but as impotent as hate has ever been.

Richard III is a "hero" drama, the drama of one man who in himself personifies the evil of the civil war. The play has no Brutus, no Cassius, no Lady Macbeth, no Iago, nobody else to share the burden or the blame, or to turn the purposes of Richard's evil will. Richard is the juggernaut going his remorseless way; the others are but the victims whom we watch as they fall. Sometimes we scarcely pity them in their calamity, for the ones who die under the wheels are of the same base kind as he who drives the chariot.

The second difference between Richard and Macbeth, Hamlet, and Othello is that the conflict in the play is entirely a conflict between the hero and someone outside himself. Richard has no inward conflict. He has no struggle against his better impulses, for all his impulses are bad. He displays no change in character, no deterioration and no sign of redemption. He ends the play as he begins—a man wholly absorbed in a consuming passion of evil purpose.

In portraying Richard, Shakespeare has done something not matched elsewhere. He has given us a man who is evil, only evil, and that continually. This picture, of course, is in the simple and classic pattern of ancient story—the division between good guys and bad guys. The books which used to delight our youth were simple. Just before "To be continued" we were wont to read: "The countryman who held the wretches in his iron grip was our hero Frank Merrywell"; and we knew that Frank Merrywell was entirely good and the wretches were entirely bad.

In his early days Shakespeare tended to follow this timeless division. But as he thought more about human life, he changed the pattern of the conflict. He made it not a struggle between good guys and bad guys but, rather, a struggle between the good and the bad impulses in the same individual. Again and again in Shakespeare's later plays one hears the echo of Paul, "The good that I would I do not: but the evil which I would not, that I do. . . . O wretched man that I am!"

In *Richard III,* however, Shakespeare was as yet concerned not with the inward struggle of divided personality but with the outward struggle of conflicting personalities. Yet nowhere else does he represent a man so entirely wicked. He has no other character who, although human, yet so resembles the cold, scoffing fiend, depicted later in Marlowe's Dr. Faustus and in Goethe's Faust: the man who has deliberately sold himself to the devil.

Needless to say, Richard the Third does not always appear evil in the play. There is much about Richard in the play, as in his life, to attract sympathy from those who know him not. Shakespeare knew that the greater peril came when the evil man was intelligent and resourceful, when he appeared as an angel of light. Richard is presented as a man of many gifts. He could be all things to all men. He could, as he boasted, seem a saint when most he played the devil, and clothe his "naked villainy with old odd ends stolen out of holy writ." Moreover, because he had no conflict with himself, he had even in his wickedness a certain inner glee. In *Henry VI* he had boasted,

> Why, I can smile, and murder whiles I smile,
> And cry "Content" to that which grieves my heart,
> And wet my cheeks with artificial tears,
> And frame my face to all occasions.
> I'll drown more sailors than the mermaid shall;
> I'll slay more gazers than the basilisk;
> I'll play the orator as well as Nestor,
> Deceive more slyly than Ulysses could,
> And, like a Sinon, take another Troy.
> I can add colours to the chameleon,
> Change shapes with Proteus for advantages,
> And set the murderous Machiavel to school.

Richard could play, with not a pause of breath between, the blusterer, the wag, the penitent, the hearty friend, the open-minded counselor. He was a consummate actor—this is why a great many actors have liked to play him. Moreover, he was brave and adventurous. His audacity, his self-possession, his presence of mind, and his courage never failed him. His final speech to his army, though he is going into defeat, has the same kind of courage possessed by a Napoleon or a Wellington. At the end he does not suicide like Brutus or Cassius, not he. He fights with reckless abandon, and he slays five Richmonds before he himself is slain, with no more thought of craving mercy than he ever had of giving it.

Richard is unchanging only in his evil purpose. He has no honor, no fear, no affection. In *Henry VI, Part III*, as he stabs the king, he says with a jeer:

> Down, down to hell; and say I sent thee thither:
> I, that have neither pity, love, nor fear.

And then he turns and adds to himself: "Clarence, thy turn is next, and then the rest."

Even earlier than this he has stabbed the wounded young prince Edward before the eyes of Edward's mother, saying to him contemptuously: "Sprawl'st thou? take that, to end thy agony." But for the king, Richard would have stabbed the mother too. "Why should she live, to fill the world with words?" As callously he kills, or causes to be killed, the fearsome procession of his subsequent victims. He passes from crime to crime without a moment of morality.

Richard is different from Macbeth. Macbeth has some honor. He honors the king. He has some love. He loves his wife. He is torn with ambition, but ambition divides a heart that is "full of the milk of human kindness." Even Lady Macbeth has a mind for that which she has no heart to perform. But Richard is the completely evil man, rejoicing in iniquity and saying, like Milton's Satan: "All good to me is lost; Evil, be thou my Good." [1]

In previous plays Shakespeare not only developed Richard's character, but he also suggested that the deep source of the moral deformity was a physical deformity. Shakespeare exag-

[1] *Paradise Lost*, Book IV, l. 109.

gerated the actual defect which gave Richard the name of "Crookback." He made Richard a monster from birth, unnatural in person and, therefore, unnatural in character. Shakespeare knew indeed that the ultimate secret was not in the defect but in Richard's response to the defect. Perhaps Shakespeare had read Bacon's essay "On Deformity" in which the first sentence declares: "Deformed persons are commonly even with nature: for as nature hath done ill by them, so do they by nature; being for the most part (as the Scripture saith) *void of natural affection*." [2] "Void of natural affection" is a precise description of Richard the Third. But Bacon saw that his introductory generalization was a half-truth. He qualified his judgment, saying: "Whosoever hath any thing fixed in his person that doth induce contempt, hath also a perpetual spur in himself to rescue and deliver himself from scorn." And, Bacon added, the manner of rescue will be "either by virtue or malice." [3]

Bacon then listed men who had done it by virtue—among others Aesop and Socrates. And we may quickly supplement Bacon's list. One thinks of such a man as William Wilberforce. When he arose to address the House of Commons, he looked like a dwarf from a fairy tale. His form, said the *London Times,* "was like the letter 's.' It resembled a stick that could not be straightened." Boswell said, "I saw . . . a mere shrimp mount the table; but as I listened, he grew and grew until the shrimp became a whale." [4]

Wilberforce delivered himself by virtue, Richard the Third by malice.

Because Richard felt himself so different from other men, he got a bitter satisfaction in being different.

[2] *Essays of Francis Bacon* (London: J. M. Dent & Sons), p. 131.
[3] *Ibid.*
[4] R. Coupland, *Wilberforce* (London: Oxford University Press, 1923), p. 4.

Then, since the heavens have shaped my body so,
Let hell make crook'd my mind to answer it.
(*Henry VI*, Part III, Act V, scene 6)

Richard found malicious delight in inverting the ways of men, in casting aside the standard by which they lived, in making wrong what others thought right and right what others thought wrong. Long afterward Nietzsche used the phrase "the transvaluation of values." But before Nietzsche put the phrase in literature, Shakespeare put the picture in art. Richard the Third was the Nietzschean superman, embodied selfishness, above all ordinary standards, beyond all moral conventions.

It is instructive to note that Shakespeare heightened Richard's iniquity by linking it with more than Richard's intelligence. He did not draw Richard more wicked than he was. Richard the Third was a monster of villainy. But Shakespeare accentuated that villainy with an unearned increment of mother wit. Shakespeare knew that the ultimate degradation of human character comes from intelligence without conscience.

Richard's calculated depravity is made all the more vivid by contrast with the untutored brutality of the two murderers whom he employed to kill his brother. They were but professional assassins; but as they went to their deed, they did feel some low stirrings of compunction. They discovered within them "certain dregs of conscience." One of them accusingly said, "It [conscience] makes a man a coward: a man cannot steal, but it accuseth him; he cannot swear, but it checks him; he cannot lie with his neighbor's wife, but it detects him: it is a blushing shamefast spirit that mutinies in a man's bosom; it fills one full of obstacles . . . it beggars any man that keeps it." The murderers sought to placate their conscience with the plea that what they did was not their wrong; it was upon command, "and he that hath commanded is the king."

84

We can hardly read the line without remembering that at the Nuremberg trial one man, whose job was to load the furnaces with human bodies all day long, made as his sufficient excuse, "I only did what I was told. It was not my responsibility." Is there any wilfulness of the heart that Shakespeare has not probed?

The murderers, in any case, are better than Richard. They have some conscience. He denies conscience. He meant what he said at the last to the army,

> Conscience is but a word that cowards use,
> Devised at first to keep the strong in awe:
> Our strong arms be our conscience, swords our law.

We might, perhaps, think that Shakespeare's delineation of Richard is exaggerated, save that in our day we have learned its truth. We remember the boast of Hermann Goering, "I have no conscience." We recall the report of Lieutenant Colonel Douglas Kelley, who was the chief psychiatrist at the Nuremberg trials. He spent eighty to ninety hours with each of the chief prisoners. He said that not one of them was, in the normal sense, demented; not one could have been locked up in an asylum. "There wasn't," said Kelley, "an insane Joe in the crowd." But, he observed, they had this in common: they were destitute of the normal conception of right and wrong. After the murder of millions they had not the slightest sense of guilt. "Rosenberg summed up their feelings when he said to me 'We shouldn't have killed six million Jews. It turned public opinion against us.' " The Nazi leaders were, to use the imagery of G. K. Chesterton, as void of the sense of guilt as a crocodile who has eaten his fourth missionary.

Shakespeare has not exaggerated. In fact, in his drama he has created Richard as a solitary monster. In our generation we have met his kind in companies.

Shakespeare's acuteness is further shown in one penetrating suggestion. Shakespeare never used the word "unconscious" with the connotations of modern psychology, but he understood well enough what modern psychologists mean. He understood that conscience was "the voice of the repressed good." He shows that though Richard has indeed denied conscience with such determined will that he has driven it from all his conscious contemplation, he has not been able to drive it from his unconscious mind. When Richard sleeps, conscience stirs.

One scene in the play is unforgettable. It is one of the most powerful scenes in all drama. It occurs in the last act, when accumulated wickedness is about to bring its fitting reward. On the night before the battle of Bosworth Field, as the king sleeps, he dreams; and in his dreams he sees the ghosts of all his victims one by one rise before him to charge him with his crimes. He hears the accusing shadows, with one voice like an echo of doom, bid him, "Despair and die." Prince Edward, whom he has stabbed; Henry, whom he has stabbed; Clarence, his brother, whom he has paid assassins to murder; Rivers, Grey, Vaughan, and Hastings, his discarded tools; Anne, his first wife; the two young princes, his nephews—all rise to speak the words he will not hear, and to tell him that "God and good angels" fight against his wickedness.

Then follows one of those strange soliloquies that only a supreme genius could imagine. It is an extraordinary piece of analysis, a pure flight of poetry matched in this play only by the dream of Clarence. Richard starts from his sleep and, with the confused utterance of a man half in the world of dreams and half in the world of day, speaks truth that awake he will not admit. Says Richard, "Have mercy, Jesu!" (What an extraordinary cry from this villain who knows no mercy, "Have mercy, Jesu!") Then he continues:

> Soft! I did but dream.
> O coward conscience, how dost thou afflict me!
> The lights burn blue. It is now dead midnight.
> Cold fearful drops stand on my trembling flesh.
> What! do I fear myself? there's none else by:
> Richard loves Richard; that is, I am I.
> Is there a murderer here? No. Yes, I am:
> Then fly: What, from myself? Great reason why:
> Lest I revenge. What! myself upon myself?
> Alack! I love myself. Wherefore? for any good
> That I myself have done unto myself?
> O! no: alas! I rather hate myself
> For hateful deeds committed by myself.
> I am a villain. Yet I lie; I am not.
> Fool, of thyself speak well: fool, do not flatter.
> My conscience hath a thousand several tongues,
> And every tongue brings in a several tale,
> And every tale condemns me for a villain.
> Perjury, perjury, in the high'st degree;
> Murder, stern murder, in the direst degree;
> All several sins, all used in each degree,
> Throng to the bar, crying all "Guilty! guilty!"
> I shall despair. There is no creature loves me;
> And if I die, no soul will pity me.

So Shakespeare pictures the unconscious mind of the man who consciously scorns conscience. When Sir Richard Ratcliff enters, Richard says, "O Ratcliff, I have dream'd a fearful dream!" "I fear, I fear,—"

> By the apostle Paul, shadows to-night
> Have struck more terror to the soul of Richard,
> Than can the substance of ten thousand soldiers.

Deny conscience if you will, says Shakespeare, you but lie to your own soul.

One further assumption pervades not only *Richard III* but also the entire cycle of the history plays. The evil men who seem so strong are weak, and they are weak because of their wickedness. There is a nemesis of greed and cruelty. They who think only of their own advantage, in the end destroy themselves. They who seem to be breaking the moral law are in process of being broken by it. And "though the mills of God grind slowly, yet they grind exceeding small."

Punishment, to be sure, as Shakespeare makes clear, is not arbitrary. God does not reach from heaven to rebuke cruel men or strike them dead. The penalty that scourges them is the inexorable consequence of their own deeds; and from that consequence there is no escape. " 'What will you have,' quoth God, 'pay for it and take it.' "

In the whole extraordinary cycle of the history plays nothing is more impressive then the terrible retribution upon those wicked men who of their own unbridled lusts and arrogant ambitions made England swim in blood. Clear as ever is written the word, as inexorable in the time of Richard the Third as in the time of Julius Caesar or Genghis Khan, Mussolini or Hitler, "There is a way which seemeth right unto a man, but the end thereof are the ways of death."

7

JULIUS CAESAR
The Tragedy of Good Intention

SHAKESPEARE wrote *Julius Caesar* after ten strenuous years of creative activity in which he had written perhaps twenty plays. He had experimented in tragedy with *Romeo and Juliet*. He had progressed from *Love's Labor's Lost* to such mature comedies as *Twelfth Night* and *As You Like It*. In addition, following a preliminary attempt with *King John* of the twelfth century, he had completed his titanic series of historical plays on fifteenth-century England: a superdrama consisting of 8 plays with 40 acts and 191 scenes, and continuing from the reign of Richard the Second through the three Henry's and Edward the Fourth to the death of Richard the Third. All this he had done in scarcely more than ten years; and he was still under thirty-five years of age.

Yet in *Julius Caesar,* Shakespeare made a distinct departure from the past. Here he entered a new adventure of the imagination. He began to meditate upon the nature of human life and the shape of human destiny as he saw it revealed in the vanished Empire of ancient Rome.

Later he was to return to the same field with *Antony and Cleopatra,* and even venture into Greece with *Pericles*. But for the moment he dealt with "the mightiest Julius" as a solitary venture. Forthwith, he turned his mind to the great tragedies. Following *Julius Caesar* he wrote *Hamlet,* and in quick succession he continued with *Othello, Macbeth,* and *King Lear.*

Julius Caesar was the gateway to a theater that was to take on new dimensions and concern itself with a new cast. Thereafter, whether in comedy or history or tragedy, Shakespeare was not merely a seventeenth-century Englishman. All the world was his stage, all time was his setting, and all his other characters were supporting players to the two chief performers: the spirit lusting against the flesh, and the flesh against the spirit.

In *Julius Caesar,* as in other historical plays, Shakespeare was true to history; but he was not bound by the annals of local events. Caesar's triumph over Pompey, for example, was celebrated in October, 45 B.C.: Shakespeare puts it at the feast of the Lupercalia, February 15, 44 B.C. Octavius did not reach Rome until two months after the assassination; Shakespeare has him in Rome immediately after Antony's funeral speech. Portia committed suicide after Brutus was defeated in battle; Shakespeare gets rid of her before the battle has begun. There were two battles of Philippi separated by twenty days; Shakespeare crowds them both into one.

Shakespeare, in fact, took a complexity of events, which in chronicle extended over three years, and in his drama compressed them within the space of six days. He almost makes one question whether in his creation he took a tip from Genesis. It is no matter. He was not interested in events; he was interested in the reason for events.

The play is constructed from a few episodes in the year 44 B.C., when Caesar, at the climax of his fame and power, was assassinated in the Senate House. To quicken our perception of the issue we should extend somewhat the range of the narrative.

Nineteen bloodstained years after Sulla the dictator of Rome had been forced to abdicate, three years after Pompey had finished his conquest of Syria and Jerusalem and Cicero had put down the conspiracy of Cataline, Caesar, Pompey, and Crassus joined forces to govern Rome in the First Triumvirate (60 B.C.).

Caesar soon departed to victorious campaigns in Gaul and Britain. He returned to find that Crassus had been killed by the Parthians and that Pompey had already begun to contend for sole power. In a daring and famous adventure Caesar crossed the Rubicon (49 B.C.) and opened war on Pompey's party. After the death of Pompey, Caesar carried his conquest to Egypt, destroyed Ptolemy, and gave the reins of authority to Cleopatra. Then he set out for Spain, where he crushed the remnants of opposition led by Ptolemy's sons. From Spain he returned again to Rome, now unchallenged conqueror. Forthwith, he assumed supreme power and made himself the Western world's first uncrowned dictator.

The superstitions of ancient days made a special divinity to hedge a king. On February 15, 44 B.C., the subservient senate tendered Caesar a crown. Caesar declined; but he seemed to observers "very loath to lay his fingers off it." A month later the rumor ran that he was to receive a second offer. As he was proceeding to the Senate House, a group of his enemies, incited by Cassius, closed in and stabbed him to death. Immediately, a rival group, headed by Antony, fomented a civil war to seize power for themselves.

Coming events cast their shadows before. Even in the play one can foresee the inevitable sequence: a second Caesar, more tyrannous than the first. Selfish and unscrupulous men supporting movements professedly in the name of freedom created a malignant chaos that destroyed freedom.

All this makes good material for a play. The incidents have been taken from ancient Rome; but the essentials are of the abiding pattern of human hope and human tragedy, and should not be obscure to those who have in this later day witnessed again the rise of totalitarian empires. As we watch, we do not find it hard to change the outward form, to give to ancient scenes a local habitation and to ancient characters a modern name.

The ruthless dictator liquidating his rivals and entrenching his power within the framework of a military state; the political opportunist using high-sounding phrases about liberty to destroy liberty; the well-meaning idealist unaware that he is being exploited by evil men for evil purpose; the jealous underlings waiting only for the moment when they can safely strike; the confused and ignorant multitude knowing that they desire liberty but blindly putting their faith in the facile demagogue who will strip from them the last shred of liberty—all these are men whose faces are familiar to our own time.

But though they are familiar to our time, they are not new to this twentieth century; they were not new to the seventeenth century. In the civilization of ancient Rome, Shakespeare found them all.

> Their roles, their goals, their naked souls,
> He knew—and drew the lot.[1]

Cassius, as he dips his hands in the blood of Caesar, exclaims:

> How many ages hence
> Shall this our lofty scene be acted over
> In states unborn and accents yet unknown!

[1] *Rudyard Kipling's Verse* (Toronto: The Copp Clark Co., 1934), p. 333.

But more significant than the immortality of the play is the immortality of the players. They still endure. This is the eternal pattern of tragedy; this "the drift of agony for ever." [2]

Julius Caesar is particularly suited for production in moving picture. Storm, thunder and the crash of battle, mob spectacles and street processions, can be lifted by the camera to a magnitude which reinforces the theme. Even with "a willing suspension of disbelief" the limits of the stage make it difficult for the spectator to be properly impressed by a momentous conflict between armies consisting of four men, and a storm manufactured off stage by someone beating a bass drum. In cumulative excitement no stage performance can match the *Julius Caesar* already presented in the movies.

Yet the screen itself, for all its magnificence, is designed, no less than the stage on which Burbage played, to testify that the things which are seen are temporal and the things which are unseen are eternal. The tempest is awesome, but it makes no difference; the outcome of the play is in no way determined by the raging of nature. The fighting is presented on impressive fields of combat; but the issue does not arise from armies and is not settled by armies. What is of consequence is happening in the hearts of men. *Julius Caesar* is not an indictment of nature or destiny; it is not a study of military strategy; it has no interest even in the Empire of Rome, save as the external show becomes setting for the conflict of souls. It is a study of men resolving into a study of man.

Let us, then, turn to the men whose passions give the play its significance. In passing we need observe only that in this play, so

[2] Christopher Fry, *A Sleep of Prisoners* (London: Oxford University Press, 1951) , p. 17.

different from certain other Shakespearean plays, the women
are of little consequence: Calpurnia is childish and is rightly
dismissed as a child. Portia impresses us more with the measure
of her self-esteem than with any obvious merit. When the going
gets tough for her husband, she commits suicide and leaves him
to face his ordeal when he knows her dead.

Let us, then, consider four of the men whose passions and
ambitions fashion the substance of drama.

First in order of appearance comes he who gives the play
its title. By many measurements Julius Caesar has a place with
the great men of all time. His strength and ability brought order to a universal empire. But he was more than a military
genius. He was a student of rhetoric and an author who has left
us a treatise on astronomy, a grammar, and commentaries that
after twenty centuries still hold their place as classics of literature. Caesar was, in ample measure, the philosopher-king of
whom Plato had dreamed. He did indeed "bestride the narrow
world like a Colossus." He gave immortality even to his enemies—for Brutus and Cassius would have been buried in ob-
livion had they not struck "the foremost man of all this world."

Shakespeare gives suggestion that he himself regarded Caesar
as "the noblest man that ever lived in the tide of times." In
three other plays he makes deferential reference to this "famous man." But in this play he is less than just to Caesar's
greatness. Perhaps he is so deliberately, both to lend dramatic
realism to the assassination and also to portray Caesar as Caesar
seemed in contemporary eyes. (Abraham Lincoln as we see him
today is far removed from the president whom Stanton thought
a fool.) At any rate, Shakespeare dresses the stage Caesar almost
in motley. He represents Caesar as vain even to insolence, the
victim of superstition, the dupe of his enemies—a man who has
perhaps been great, but who is already poisoned by the corrup-

tion of power; and who in terms of ancient times is scorned of the gods and left with fate: the destiny his nature fashions.

From Caesar let us turn to Brutus. Brutus is a philosopher, but not a philosopher-king. Brutus was indeed "the noblest Roman of them all":

> All the conspirators, save only he,
> Did that they did in envy of great Caesar;
> He only, in a general honest thought
> And common good to all, made one of them.
> His life was gentle, and the elements
> So mix'd in him that Nature might stand up
> And say to all the world "This was a man!"

Brutus came of noble lineage. Five hundred years before, as the grateful Romans well remembered, a Brutus had driven the first tyrant from Rome and had become the founding father of the Republic. Brutus, moreover, was linked in the public mind with his father-in-law, Cato the Younger, the philosopher who had been accounted "the conscience of Rome," and who, when Caesar usurped the ancient rights of the Republic, startled the citizens by committing suicide as a gesture of protest.

In an age of despotism and corruption Brutus was a man of personal gentleness and irreproachable integrity. In the play we see him thoughtful of his page boy, kind to his bondsman, and even in his power "armed so strong in honesty" that he would rather "coin [his] heart" than support his cause "by vile means," or "any indirection."

Brutus was a fighter only by necessity, a scholar by inclination. Late at night, even though he is weary and awaiting a day of battle, he pulls his precious book from his pocket and for a moment leaves the place of intrigue and conflict for the regions of the imagination. We remember General Wavell, during

World War II, reading Browning in the campaigns of North Africa and the Far East. We remember also Abraham Lincoln, relieving the desperate hours of the Civil War by reading to his cabinet the essays of Artemus Ward. Probably, however, Brutus would not be carrying a book of humor. Brutus is almost self-consciously noble. Even in announcing the death of Portia, he includes a description of himself, "No man bears sorrow better."

But whatever his defects, Brutus was "an honourable man"; and not all the cunning of an unscrupulous enemy can steal the worth from that judgment. Brutus is not to be despised; he is to be pitied. Therein lies the heart of the tragedy.

Brutus was that typically ineffective man, the "saint in politics." Because he knows that his *purposes* are sincere, he cannot see that his *plans* are foolish. Because his actions are suffused with virtue, he cannot believe that they are being twisted to evil ends. Because he has dedicated himself to a high cause, he cannot see that he is no more than a tool of men who would destroy all that he cherishes. The essence of the tragedy is that the passion for liberty in the heart of a good man can become the instrument to enthrone a lasting tyranny.

Cassius is simpler and easier to know. He is an unprincipled egotist. He is bitter and cynical, believing that all men can be bought by those who know the price. He is full of consuming ambition and corroding jealousy of all who would outsoar his flight. Caesar rightly judges:

> Such men as he be never at heart's ease
> Whiles they behold a greater than themselves,
> And therefore are they very dangerous.

Cassius had unwisely sided with Pompey; but after defeat in battle, he had, by the magnanimity of Caesar, not only been pardoned but also made praetor. Yet he continued to hate the man who spared his life and gave him honor. He was nursing ambitions as vast as Caesar's, unsupported by abilities as great. The evil he saw in Caesar mirrored the evil he hid in his own heart.

The fourth significant character is Mark Antony. Antony, like Richard the Third, appears in two plays and is described more fully in the second. In *Julius Caesar,* Antony is as yet a youthful soldier of fortune, a reckless hothead who "revels long a-nights," and is "given to sports, to wildness and much company." He is an opportunist, eager to jump at the most reckless chance. But as yet he has certain redeeming features. In *Antony and Cleopatra* we see his native aptitude for vice nurtured to full-grown sensuality by the Sorceress of the Nile.

In his first allegiance Antony had been more fortunate than Cassius. He had thrown in his fortunes with Caesar; and was devoted to Caesar, as later henchmen of his kind have been devoted to Hitler and Stalin. But Antony's devotion to Caesar had its roots in his own advantage. The Bible says, "Faithful are the wounds of a friend." Antony would never inflict such wounds. He supported all the worst in Caesar, including the ambition to be king. In every event his only concern was to seize the main chance for himself.

The whole of Shakespeare scarcely provides another shift of scene more significant than that in *Julius Caesar* between the end of the third act and the opening of the fourth. In the third act Antony is, to all appearances, the apologist of justice, the exponent of pity, the champion of the people, the enemy of treason and of tyranny. Even then Shakespeare lets us see that all this is pretense, that Antony is no more than a smooth-tongued adventurer, here as everywhere exploiting every turn of events for his own good fortune. As he watches the maddened mob rush away to senseless destruction, he drops his pose of public concern and exclaims with cynical glee:

> Now let it work. Mischief, thou art afoot,
> Take thou what course thou wilt
>
> . . . .
>
> Fortune is merry,
> And in this mood will give us anything.

Then the fourth act opens to present Antony no longer the public orator but now the man of power. He is talking with Octavius and Lepidus, planning the mastery of Rome. He stands not now upon such slippery ground as he has so recently known. The revolt is going well. Antony needs no longer to pretend, and he quickly reveals his true nature.

As the curtain rises, Antony speaks, "These many then shall die." He is planning to consolidate his power with a blood purge. Callously he calls for the death of the brother of Lepidus, and just as callously pays the price by marking next his own nephew. With a jest worthy of the French Revolution, Antony says: "He shall not live; look, with a spot I damn him." Then as Lepidus leaves, Antony quickly turns to Octavius and proposes that as soon as convenient the two of them get rid of Lepidus and divide the power between themselves.

The scene has the more impact upon our imagination because we know as we watch that Octavius will follow Antony's suggestion. He will get rid of Lepidus; but he will not stop there. He will go right on to get rid of Antony. And the second Caesar will stand as the first, to "bear the palm alone."

We need mention no other individual in the play, but we should make mention of the mob. The first scene of the first act brings clear suggestion that a people so unstable, so easily swayed, so ignorant of the things that belong unto their peace, cannot save themselves from tyranny. Their feelings are, in the main, right. They have a certain pride in the traditions of the Republic. But they have not the character to sustain the traditions. They have been spoiled by the bread and circuses with which greedy rulers have bought their favor. They are easily persuaded by Antony to rise in mutiny. But what do they do? They rush out in mad fury and kill an innocent man. They know that he is an innocent man. He is Cinna the poet, but he bears the same name as Cinna the conspirator. (Guilt by association is not only of the twentieth century.) He will serve as outlet for their passions. As children in temper would mutilate a doll, they tear him limb from limb.

The mob in *Julius Caesar* bears witness that no matter who talks of giving freedom to a people, the only people who can be free are those who are fit for freedom. The others of their own folly will deliver themselves to demagogues, and their last state will be worse than the first.

What, then, is the pattern of tragedy that *Julius Caesar* presents? The play is Shakespeare's reflection upon the natural war which has in varying degrees existed in civilization after civilization between the strength of autocracy and the idea of liberty. In the persons of Caesar, Brutus, Antony, and the others, Shakespeare shows why tyrants who are in the wrong are not always conquered by crusades which are in the right, why a great cause may fall away from the noble ideals which gave it birth.

The heart of the tragedy, which has repeated itself wearily through the ages, is pictured in Brutus and the fall of the Republic at his death. Brutus exemplifies in himself all the worthy aims and ideals of the democracy which he cherishes, yet he brings calamity upon himself, his cause, and his nation.

99

Caesar may be self-seeking, but Caesar can govern. Brutus is not self-seeking, but Brutus cannot govern. Brutus is the kind of man who in a democracy can be excellent in opposition but is disastrous in power. In opposition he can be the conscience of the nation. In power he does not know the prudent maxim "Politics is the art of the possible."

Honest, idealistic Brutus is spectacularly foolish in his estimate of political possibilities. He has no inkling of the gulf between abstract ideas of liberty and practical problems of democracy. In his study he idealizes the common people out of all reality. He thinks that if they can be free, they will naturally be virtuous. As soon as Caesar is dead, Brutus makes a foolish speech and then turns the mob over to Mark Antony. He cries, "Peace," when there is no peace. He thinks that since the tyrant has been killed, freedom is therefore secure. He goes home happily to tell it all to Portia. But before he understands what has happened, the populace whom he has so idealized is lusting for his blood. Before he has time to be a statesman, he has become a fugitive.

In 1789 a distinguished American wrote from Paris to George Washington giving his impression of Louis XVI, "He is an amiable and upright man, as doubtless would have made a fine minister in peace time, but his ancestors have bequeathed him a Revolution." [3] Brutus might have made a fine prime minister in a mature democracy; but his ancestors have bequeathed him a revolution, and Brutus is not equal to a revolution. He is not equal to creating or defending a democracy; he is equal only to dreaming about it. Few men bring more genuine danger to democracy than the unselfish idealist who becomes the front man for the unscrupulous schemer.

[3] Halford E. Luccock, *Christian Faith and Economic Change* (New York: The Abingdon Press, 1936), p. 19.

Brutus, in fact, timelessly illustrates that the survival of democracy demands more than spiritual ideals. It demands children of light who on the earthly level of practical politics can meet and overcome the children of darkness. In the tensions of human society good people who are devoted to good causes often frustrate their own purposes. Temperance advocates are sometimes the liquor trade's soundest assets: they will drive anyone to drink. Missionary enthusiasts sometimes are enough to make us pray that the heathen become not such as they. Politicians are sometimes so timid and incompetent that they play directly into the hands of an Aberhart, a Huey Long, or a Hitler. No personal virtue in democratic leaders can compensate for administrative incapacity.

It is wrong to have wicked people composing a church choir, yet to have a good choir it is not enough to have good people; it is essential to have people who can sing. It is calamitous to have dictators in government, yet if we are to have an ordered society, it is not enough that political leaders be pious; it is essential that they be able to govern. Brutus, with the will to restore liberty, is incompetent in leadership. He can assassinate Caesar, but he cannot save the Republic.

The play, therefore, is rightly called *Julius Caesar*. Caesar goes, and sees not, but he still conquers. He has only a minor place on the stage. He appears only on three occasions, and he speaks only 150 lines. His dead body is lying on the floor in two scenes, each of which takes a longer time than the living Caesar required for every word he uttered. Yet Caesar conquers, for Caesarism conquers.

It is said that in Berlin during the last days when the Nazi empire was falling in flames and ruin, Adolf Hitler said in a defiant frenzy, "Put on the graves of the dead German soldiers, this phrase: *And Yet You Were Victorious.*" Hitler's defiance was not without hope nor without insight. Hitler can be conquered, yet Hitlerism conquer. A totalitarian nation—either in cold war or hot—can be conquered, yet totalitarianism conquer. Caesar can be stabbed to death but in death be stronger than in life. At the end Brutus rightly exclaimed:

> O Julius Caesar, thou art mighty yet!
> Thy spirit walks abroad.

Brutus and his fellow conspirators had no capacity to make the people independent of a Caesar. They had not among them even a uniting principle, save the desire to throw the rascal out and get themselves in. They had no cohesion, save the cohesion of a wolf pack. Their contradictory chatter after the assassination and the foolish aimless anger of the mob, prophesied all too clearly the doom of democracy. Caesar, said Cassius, would not have been a wolf, but that he saw the Romans were but sheep. They were still sheep—now with childish, confused shepherds running in every direction. Nothing more was needed to invite another Caesar.

The pattern of history is inexorable. The greed of Antony signed his own death warrant. The folly of Brutus signed his party's death warrant. Octavius eliminated every rival and emerged a second Caesar. Promptly he turned the Republic into a monarchy and without the hesitation of Julius proclaimed himself emperor. He gave himself the title of Augustus and, not content to be acknowledged as king, decreed that he be worshipped as god. He became first of a line of tyrants which, continuing through Tiberius, Caligula, Claudius, and Nero, maintained a worsening despotism until the Empire of Rome collapsed through its own corruption. Brutus, who would restore liberty, succeeded only in establishing a lasting tyranny. Caesarism conquered.

And—even in historical drama—Caesarism conquered not because of outward things, but because of inward things; not because of storm or battle, but because of the stupid greed of the populace, the evil in Cassius and Antony, and the inward defect in Brutus. In *Julius Caesar,* as always in Shakespeare, men are not the creatures of circumstance; they are the creators of circumstance. In *Julius Caesar,* as always in Shakespeare, destiny is the imprint of character.

8

THE MERCHANT OF VENICE
The Tragedy of Inhumanity

WE NOW turn to a play which is different from any we have previously considered—*The Merchant of Venice*. It is a comedy. Comedy does not indicate farce, but, technically, a play wherein the dilemma is resolved in what is judged to be a happy solution.

To this degree *The Merchant of Venice* is comedy. It has not a murder or a suicide or a single corpse. In one of the two main sections Bassanio wins the beautiful heiress Portia. In the other he saves his friend from threatened death. Also, the supporting parts—the rings story, the moonlight love scene, the buffoonery of Launcelot Gobbo—are light and diverting, and help carry the prevailing atmosphere of comedy. Had the main stories been turned into tragedy—as with the slightest alteration they might have been—then corresponding changes would have been required in the supporting parts. *The Merchant of Venice,* therefore, is properly called comedy. But it is more. It intersperses the white keys of comedy with the black keys of tragedy. In its development it speaks as seriously as any play called tragic.

The Merchant of Venice rivals *Hamlet* as the most popular of all Shakespeare's plays. Indeed, to large numbers of people *The Merchant of Venice* is Shakespeare. This is a modern development. Significantly, the comedy has achieved this position only with the revival of its tragic element. For generations Shylock was played as a comic figure, the butt of public scorn and obloquy. With his red beard, copied from the time of Burbage, he was portrayed as a contemptible old man completely obsessed with the twin passions of avarice and revenge —ugly, not as Richard the Third was ugly, with physical deformity; but, rather, with mental deformity.

It was not until the coming of such great actors as Macklin in the eighteenth century and Kean and Irving in the nineteenth that Shylock came on the stage with qualities that generations had forgotten. Such actors portrayed Shylock as a man who was bitter, but who had been made bitter by injustice; who was fired by hatred that was irrational and indefensible, but not more irrational and indefensible than the Christian scorn by which it was nurtured. He was pictured, in brief, as a man who was wrong, but who had been wronged; a man who even in the midst of calamity in a measure just, yet constituted a protest against oppression and shame that were wholly unjust. He embodied an immortal appeal to elemental dignity and rights which he had been shamelessly denied.

To present such a Shylock was to do no more than to restore what Shakespeare had originally created. There was truth in the couplet which Pope wrote after seeing Macklin's first performance:

> This is the Jew
> That Shakespeare drew.

The play, of course, is more than Shylock. It is a union of two ancient folk tales with lineage not only in English but also in Spanish and Greek and other folk literature: the story of the pound of flesh demanded as payment for a bond; and the story of the three caskets which hid the secret needed to win a beautiful heiress. Significantly, these two stories, so different, were not just old; but, as though there were some chemical affinity between them, they had already been combined in a play presented in England when Shakespeare was about fifteen years of age. As though these two stories did not themselves produce sufficient complications, Shakespeare added two minor stories: one about an elopement, the other about the mishandling of some wedding rings—all this and Launcelot Gobbo, one of the most diverting of Shakespeare's fools.

These various stories are interwoven in the following manner: Bassanio, an improvident young gentleman of Venice, wishes to marry the richest heiress of his day, Portia of Belmont. He is even in love with her, no difficult task. He may not have heard, but he knows the wisdom of the Scottish counsel: "My son, don't marry for money; but marry where money is." Bassanio has not had the privilege of seeing the modern moving picture which deals with the reverse problem of getting a rich husband. But Bassanio does understand what even the blindest of the young women in that picture can see, that money is a powerful help in marrying money. So to get the money to pay proper court to Portia, he turns for help to his generous friend Antonio, a merchant of Venice.

It happens that for the time Antonio's assets are all tied up with cargoes at sea. However, for the sake of his friend—all the world loves a lover, particularly a lover about to land a fortune—Antonio breaks his customary rule and seeks the required sum from a Jewish moneylender. Antonio makes no secret of the fact that he despises the man whose help he solicits; and Shylock makes no less secret of the fact that he returns Antonio's contempt—as a moneylender might be excused for doing—with considerable interest.

When Antonio makes application for the large sum of money, Shylock asks him how he might be expected to reply to such a request:

> Fair sir, you spit on me on Wednesday last;
> You spurn'd me such a day; another time
> You call'd me dog; and for these courtesies
> I'll lend you thus much money?

Antonio replies:

> I am as like to call thee so again,
> To spit on thee again, to spurn thee too.

Rudely he asks Shylock to lend money, not as to a friend, but as to an enemy. In reply Shylock, changing his tone, says that he will forget the shames and lend the money, and "in a merry sport" ask only that if the money be not repaid, Antonio forfeit a pound of his own flesh. Bassanio, in alarm, protests such terms; but Antonio, as contemptuous as ever of the man whose aid he seeks, says with foolish complacency that the terms do not matter, because all his ships will have come to port long before the money is due.

The scene now shifts from Venice to Belmont, where Portia in her palatial home receives her suitors. She has accepted the provision of her father's will that she marry the man who makes the right choice among three caskets, respectively of gold, silver, and lead. The prince of Morocco chooses the gold one with the inscription promising "what many men desire." The prince of Arragon—probably suggesting "arrogant"—chooses the silver one, which promises "as much as he deserves." Bassanio chooses the lead one—it is easy to be satisfied with a lead casket when the winner gets all of Portia's gold—which bears the warning,

"Who chooseth me must give and hazard all he hath." Bassanio, of course, makes the right choice and wins the lovely—and wealthy—Portia.

By this time the play is bursting out all over in a very spring-time of romance. "In the Spring a young man's fancy lightly turns to—what the girls have been thinking about all winter." Bassanio's friend Gratiano falls in love with Portia's companion, Nerissa; and another friend, Lorenzo, falls in love with Shylock's pretty daughter, Jessica. Then, while all hearts beat happily, suddenly, as on the night before Waterloo, "a deep sound strikes like a rising knell." Antonio sends a messenger saying that his ships have been lost at sea, that he cannot meet the bond, and that, though his friends have offered to pay Shylock ten times the amount due, the implacable old man is determined to invoke the stern Venetian law and demand the dread forfeit of the pound of flesh.

In the emergency Portia takes over. (After all, her attractiveness has caused all the trouble.) Hastily, she completes the marriages between herself and Bassanio and between Gratiano and Nerissa. Then she sends the two men off to Venice with enough gold to pay Antonio's debt twenty times over. Once the men are out of the way, Portia, in true womanly fashion, sets about her real designs.

By the connivance of her cousin, an influential lawyer, she arranges that, in the disguise of a distinguished doctor of law, she will be introduced to the duke of Venice and installed in the court as a judge, with Nerissa, also disguised, acting as her clerk. As judge of the court, Portia supports the precise letter of Venetian law and acknowledges the right of Shylock to exact the terms Antonio has signed.

Shylock fawns upon her for her excellent wisdom but spurns her plea when she adds that the creditor can demand justice but may choose mercy. Shylock has only one reply, "It is not in the bond." Even to Portia's request that he have a physician to stay the blood lest Antonio die, he implacably responds, " 'Tis not in the bond." So the court of Venice grants the alien plaintiff judgment against its own citizen. "The law allows it, and the court awards it."

Then, abruptly, in the very moment of Shylock's triumph, the young judge proceeds calmly to one further stipulation which is just as technical as those which have supported Shylock, but which destroys at one stroke every possibility of executing his design, and instead leaves Shylock himself in acute peril. Shylock may indeed, says the judge, take his pound of flesh; but if in the cutting he sheds "one drop of Christian blood," his lands and goods are forfeit to the state of Venice. Moreover, if he take anything save the precise exaction of the bond, more or less by the "estimation of a hair," he dies and all his goods "are confiscate." Further, as Shylock, foiled of his revenge, prepares to leave, the judge relentlessly proceeds to add that, in any case, because Shylock has manifestly conspired against the life of a citizen, half of his goods go in fine to the state and half to the citizen against whom he has so conspired. And his life lies at the will of the duke and depends solely upon that quality of mercy which he himself has spurned.

Shylock's defeat is utter. But the duke pardons the old man; and Antonio, while refusing his share, insists that Shylock write a will leaving all his estate to his daughter and that

> for this favour
> He presently become a Christian.

In the most unnatural act of all the play, Shylock agrees even to this last stipulation and departs from the court leaving Bassanio and Antonio in triumph.

With the court scene ended, the play returns quickly to the

atmosphere of comedy. Portia waives the legal fee that she could have exacted, and instead she and Nerissa demand the rings that the men have promised their wives never to lose. In recognition of their debt the men feel they can do no other. But, at home again, they are teased about their loss until Portia reveals that she was the judge and Nerissa the clerk. Then, to make all end happily, she presents a letter saying that by unexpected good fortune Antonio's ships have safely arrived in port.

All this is sheer fantasy. It is as far from reality as, say, *Peter Pan* or *Dear Brutus* or *Outward Bound*. It is less a story than a fairy tale, where truth need have no correspondence with reality.

The improbability is concerned not so much with the pound of flesh. Mutilation as a penalty did not seem nearly so far-fetched in Shakespeare's time as it does in ours. The safety of the human body has not been in the past an inviolable right. In the ancient tables of Roman law the creditor was entitled to mutilate the negligent debtor. The worth of an eye or an ear or any portion of the body, if the creditor took them in lieu of money, were stated in terms as precise as those of a present-day insurance policy. It is true that the Romans abolished these laws even before Christian times, but modifications persisted for many centuries. In medieval Europe many a person who had written something of offense to church or state had to forfeit a hand; and others who had heard and repeated some offending word lost an ear or tongue. Even down to our own lifetime Leopold of Belgium sanctioned in Africa the penalty of cutting off the hands of the natives. In Saudi Arabia the same penalty is still permitted for theft, though seldom exacted.

As to a bond—in Shakespeare's own lifetime a merchant in Venice, on hearing the tidings that Sir Francis Drake had captured San Domingo, bet a pound of his flesh that the news was not true and formally recorded the bet before a notary. (The bet after all was little more absurd than some that have been made in our own day.)

The improbabilities of the play are of a different kind. Consider, for example. the pretense—so false, yet so familiar to Shakespeare—that Portia and Nerissa in the garb of lawyers would be totally unrecognizable to their husbands. Consider also the pretense that a girl disguised as a non-existent authority on law could preside over an important court and have her judgment considered valid. Consider further a discrepancy of a different nature in the portrayal of Jessica. When one remembers the strength of affection which through centuries has characteristically marked the Jewish family, Jessica as a Jewish daughter seems wholly out of character. The wilful young woman who deceives and robs her father is, in the cold light of analysis, a wicked young woman. Yet in the play continually (and particularly in a romantic interlude of moonlight) she is altogether charming—as in such circumstances wicked young women often are.

The astonishing truth is that the play, shot through with such anomalies, is a triumph of dramatic skill. The stories are woven together so deftly, the successive scenes so relieve and complement each other, that there is not a jar or a hitch from beginning to end. At the opening Antonio with his sadness invokes a mood which brings presentiment of trouble; and at the end the lyric beauty of the moonlight scene with Lorenzo and Jessica lifts us from the fret and strain of sordid animosities to the fairyland of romance. The flight of poetry following, "The moon shines bright: in such a night as this . . .", is one of the loveliest passages in all Shakespeare.

The Merchant of Venice, as I have said, is a fairy story. It cannot be judged by realistic standards. It is, as John Middleton Murry says, an art form older than art itself, and hence appeals like all fairy stories to something deep and primitive within us. Yet, like many a fairy story, it hides not only a form that is ageless but also a truth that is eternal.

What Shakespeare did in *The Merchant of Venice* is what he did in many another play. He took old material and injected into it a new idea. In *The Merchant of Venice* the new idea is found in the character of Shylock.

We may assume that Shakespeare was not unfamiliar with the history that made the Jewish moneylender a familiar character and an inevitable villain. In Europe systematic persecution of Jews was a relatively late phenomenon. It was one of the unsavory products of the Crusades. Before the time of the Crusades, Jews in Christian Europe had lived in comparative tranquility. With the Crusades, rationally, they should have come into new favor because of the spiritual affinity of Jewish and Christian faith. Instead, in the irrational way of hatred, the fierce passions fomented against the infidels who held the Holy Sepulcher, found a convenient outlet in people nearer at hand and a great deal safer to attack. Jews were made objects of hostility on the grounds that their ancestors had crucified Christ. This was about as rational as for other peoples today to persecute Americans because their ancestors killed Abraham Lincoln. But prejudice knows no logic, and all over Christendom the preaching of the Crusades was followed by attacks upon the Jews. And the persecution so generated was to continue long after the last Crusade had dwindled to its ignominious end.

Between the first and the third Crusade, that is between the eleventh and the thirteenth centuries, there grew up the grotesque myths which branded the Jews as enemies of God, Christianity, and mankind. Then arose the legend of the Wandering Jew; and the charge of ritual murder, repeated, for example, by the prioress in Chaucer's *Canterbury Tales*. This charge, ironically, was a resurrection of an old accusation which, because of the sacraments, had in the first centuries been circulated against the Christians. By the middle of the thirteenth century, Christendom in its treatment of the Jews had reached a depth of depravity which it did not touch again till the time of Hitler's Germany. The Jews were a proscribed people, compelled to wear characteristic garb: the pointed hat and the yellow ring. Ghettos became a feature of every European city, though the name itself did not appear till the fifteenth century in Venice.

England's record was little better than that of continental nations. William the Conqueror brought the pattern of persecution from France, and, thereafter, the lot of Jews in England was bitter. Finally, in the epidemic intolerance of the thirteenth century, Jews were expelled from England and were not allowed to return until the time of Cromwell. Hence, the Jew in Shakespeare's play is of Venice and not of London. In London the Jew was unknown. He was as remote as the Moslem infidel—and as mythical, and as real, as the Devil.

We cannot understand *The Merchant of Venice* unless we understand Shylock's background and know the public to which he was presented. Shakespeare knew the popular mind. He knew how futile it would have been, even had he desired, to present, as Lessing did later with his *Nathan the Wise,* a Jew invested with all the virtue and magnanimity of a Hebrew prophet and to make such a Jew an apologist for the Jewish faith and nation. Shakespeare did something greater and more effective. With the realism that he preserves even in the midst of his most farfetched fantasy, he presented not a prophet but a Jew as he was—persecuted, scorned, embittered, schooled by Christians in hatred and able to better the instruction. Yet when the play is finished, Shakespeare has, in a manner that even the illiterate groundlings of the pit can understand, vested Shylock with new proportions, proportions that rightly discerned are no less rebuke to the Christian than to the Jew.

It is this shift of proportion that is important in *The Merchant of Venice;* and we can dismiss other considerations of the play and come to grips with the issues it creates.

First, we may note that in this play Shakespeare makes a strange departure. In other plays he suggests that what matters is what happens to people of high estate, to nobles, and to kings. As he gained experience in playwriting, he did begin to include people of lesser estate. For example, Sir John Falstaff, of the lowest order of knights, in *Henry IV*; and Nick Bottom, the weaver, in *A Midsummer-Night's Dream.* In *The Merchant of Venice,* however, he does something of which elsewhere he has no more than a suggestion. He not only makes an important character out of an alien and an outlaw; he also makes the drama a passionate plea for the underling, for the human dignity even of a man made hard and cruel by savage persecution.

How important this is appears when we consider what might have been. Shylock might, like Marlowe's *Jew of Malta,* have fitted into the ridiculous pattern of popular myth. He might have been a mess of the contemptible like Falstaff and Bottom. He might have groveled and danced and whined and lamented. But despite his bitterness, despite his vindictiveness, Shylock is, at least, never weak nor contemptible. True, he loves his gold, as well he might. He has been able to wrest from dreadful circumstances no other symbol of victory. He has no landed estates as Portia has; he has no ships at sea as Antonio has; he has no place in public honor; he has no position in affairs of state; he is, at best, no more than a tolerated alien. He has but one witness of his strength and his worth; his ducats and his jewels. Shylock has learned the truth in our cynical modern song "Diamonds Are a Girl's Best Friend."

But Shylock is no miser. When he is offered twenty times the amount of his bond, he spurns the offer. He is troubled not really about money; he is troubled about his right and dignity as a human being. In all the play he breaks only once, when he learns that his daughter has robbed him and run away to marry a Christian. Significantly, in that moment of weakness he is not presented to the audience. He is but reported, and reported by a man who hates him. Shylock himself brings his grief to the stage only in the presence of his countryman Tubal; and then it is to say that he would sooner see his daughter dead and the money in her coffin.

Shakespeare, then, makes no attempt, as dramatists in our day might have done, to present Shylock as altogether noble and his persecutors as altogether blameable. We are familiar with writers to whom the underdog is always right and the top-dog is always wrong, the rebel is always a patriot and the ruler is always a tyrant, the have-nots are wholly idealistic and the haves are completely greedy. Shakespeare knows better. He knows that even the exploited and the persecuted are not by oppression purified of culpability. He sees that Shylock's persecutors are, in large degree, unconscious of the measure of injustice they mete out to him, while Shylock is perfectly aware of the measure of hate which he returns to them and, therefore, in this respect is worse than they. He sees that Shylock by spurning mercy is himself condemned, not only by the court of Venice, but also by the abiding principles of Hebrew faith. But he also sees that though wrong, Shylock is wronged; and that despite the elaborate pretense of the court, the Jew gets neither justice nor mercy. He shows the Jew as oppressed, but he makes the oppressed Jew a protest against all oppression.

When Salarino asks Shylock why he exacts a pound of flesh, Shylock replies in terms with which great actors have always made a tremendous impact upon their audiences:

I am a Jew. Hath not a Jew eyes? hath not a Jew hands, organs, dimensions, senses, affections, passions? fed with the same food, hurt with the same weapons, subject to the same diseases, healed by the same means, warmed and cooled by the same winter and summer, as a Christian is? If you prick us, do we not bleed? if you tickle us, do we not laugh? if you poison us, do we not die? and if you wrong us, shall we not revenge? if we are like you in the rest, we will resemble you in that.

This tremendous plea becomes something like a statement of the equal rights of man—presented not in a treatise or a philosophic argument but in a fashion in which every hearer is compelled for the moment to identify himself with the sufferer.

Moreover, it is important to note how Shylock develops his argument. When he is challenged with the theory that it is wrong to injure a human being by taking from him a pound of flesh, Shylock says in reply:

> You have among you many a purchased slave,
> Which, like your asses and your dogs and mules,
> You use in abject and in slavish parts,
> Because you bought them: shall I say to you,
> Let them be free, marry them to your heirs?
> Why sweat they under burthens? let their beds
> Be made as soft as yours, and let their palates
> Be season'd with such viands? You will answer
> "The slaves are ours:" so do I answer you:
> The pound of flesh, which I demand of him,
> Is dearly bought; 'tis mine and I will have it.

Shakespeare, that is, presents what Shylock does as wrong, but as wrong not in the sense in which he is distinctive from Christians—rather, as part of a larger wrong. The injustice and mercilessness are the reflection of a wider injustice and mercilessness in the Christian world in which the Jew has to live. In

116

The Merchant of Venice, to a degree unique in all his drama, Shakespeare creates sympathy for the person in lower estate as against the person in higher estate, and makes of Shylock an incarnate plea for universal justice.

In the court scene particularly, Shakespeare throws powerful light upon the realities of Shylock's position. There he represents Shylock at his evil worst. There he pictures Shylock's Christian opponents making ostentatious parade of the impartiality of Christian law. There, also, Shakespeare makes us see that she who holds the scales of justice is blind.

To be sure, in some degree Portia herself worthily represents justice. She does not defend Shylock, but neither does she insult him or scorn him. She has magnanimity that is above prejudice. Indeed, even before the court scene, she has given indication of her mind. When the dark-skinned prince of Morocco comes to seek her hand in marriage, he is at first afraid that Portia will resent the fact that his skin is of a different color. Portia, with dignity, replies that as for color he stands as fair for her affections as any other. She declares herself ready to marry a Moor; and thus, in typical Shakespearean fashion, foreshadows the later play where Desdemona marries Othello. Portia represents justice. Having made this clear, Shakespeare makes it clear also that Portia has no place in the court of Venice.

To begin with, she is not the person she pretends to be. Her presence makes the whole proceedings illegal and, indeed, trifles with the dignity of law. Moreover, as wife of Bassanio, she is related to a man who is interested in the suit; and at the end she does not require Bassanio to pay the Jew her own three thousand ducats.

Her judgment, as well as her presence, is far removed from propriety. Shylock, she says, may take his pound of flesh; but if in the cutting he take less or more "but in the estimation of a hair," he is sentenced to death. Perhaps he may not take more, but has there ever been any law, anywhere, any time, that prevented a creditor from taking less than the full amount that he could legally demand?

The stipulation that Shylock has the right to take a pound of flesh but not to shed a drop of blood is equally absurd. In any system of law it may be accepted as an elementary principle that the legal justification of a specific action necessarily includes the natural and inescapable consequence of the action. What court would entertain the contention that a doctor with a perfect right to take out an appendix had no right to cut the skin?

Shakespeare, who is far too acute to do such a thing by accident, makes the trial scene a bitter satire of a court of justice. He presents the accusing truth that the Jew of the Middle Ages met a pretense of law only to be cheated of justice. When Shylock walks silently away, Antonio, for all his Christian contempt, is still possessed of all his riches; Bassanio, Portia, Gratiano, Nerissa, Lorenzo, Jessica, are all in the high tide of fortune; and the Jew has nothing. He has been stripped of his family, his fortune, and his faith.

"The most unkindest cut of all" (*Julius Caesar,* Act III, scene 2), false both to Jew and to Christian, is Shylock's enforced repudiation of his faith and his acceptance of Christianity. Here, to be sure, Shakespeare conformed to the conventional pattern. The English version of *The Wandering Jew* ends by having the Jew become converted to Christianity and take the name of Joseph, the father of Jesus. Thus, he shakes off Judaism and with it the eternal curse.

So Christians had thought; so Shakespeare had read. But had not Shakespeare also read, for example, in the book of Maccabees how a Jewish mother watched her seven sons, one after another, being tortured to death; and how when only her youngest was left she still defied the counsel of the king and exhorted

118

her son to stand fast in the faith? Did Shakespeare not know of the Jews in the Middle Ages who had as tenaciously clung to the faith of their fathers, or indeed of the Jews who for equal fidelity had been outlawed from England? A Jew inflamed with the fierce pride and fanatical devotion of Shylock would have had all his flesh cut from him in ounces rather than tamely submit to becoming a Christian. The forced conversion is equally false to the pride of the Jew and to the faith of the Christian.

Shakespeare could not have been unaware of the satire in making this solution agreeable to Christians. Conversion rightly means a change to other ways. The conversion of Shylock seems to mean only a change to another company. The bitterness, the hatred, the avarice, and the bigotry that have been so wrong in Shylock the Jew will, apparently, not be noticeable in Shylock the Christian.

Even in his exit, therefore, Shylock maintains an immortal appeal against the enormity of his wrongs. He is not in the true sense a Shakespearean hero, but equally he is not a Shakespearean villain. He is culpable because he fights a just fight with unjust means; he is immortal because as Victor Hugo said, when he lost his own cause, he gained the cause of his people.

It is, therefore, grievously unwise when Jewish groups try to ban *The Merchant of Venice* on the grounds that it will stimulate anti-Semitism. To begin with, the principle is wrong. To put a ban on *Oliver Twist* because Jews dislike it is to prepare for a ban on *Martin Luther* because Roman Catholics dislike it. It is to lay the ground for a ban on Jehovah's Witnesses in Quebec and on Presbyterians and Methodists in Italy and Spain. Ultimately, it is to hand to someone else a ban to be used against the Jews themselves.

Even had Shakespeare presented someone like Marlowe's *Jew of Malta,* it would still be as wrong to ban *The Merchant of Venice* because it contained an evil Jew, as it would be to ban *Richard III* because it contained an evil Englishman. But Shakespeare's play is radically different from Marlowe's. Rightly presented, it is a powerful plea, not only for the Jew, but also for every human being. There is no more reason for a Jewish actor to refuse to play Shylock than for a Negro to refuse to play Othello. Those who fear anti-Semitism might well endeavor to have *The Merchant of Venice* played with real insight before every citizen in the land.

The Merchant of Venice, then, is comedy—indeed, most diverting comedy; but it is more than comedy. It says something that we need to hear, and that we need to say again, at this time and indeed at all times. I recall an address I made some time ago when the persecution of Jews in Nazi Germany was at its evil worst. As I came to the end, I said:

What is done to the Jew will in time be done to others. What is permitted to the Jew will in time be visited upon the Gentiles. Eternally true is the principle that if tyranny, cruelty, viciousness be the pattern in dealing with one group, it will soon be the pattern in dealing with other groups. It will end by being the pattern in dealing with all. For this age speaks with thundering voice, the word true in all ages, "There will be no safety nor peace, no freedom nor justice . . . for any one, anywhere, until there can be safety, peace, freedom and justice . . . for all the children of God."

What I said then was akin to what Shylock says when he declares that to deny him justice would be to bring a danger to the charter and the city's freedom. What I said then, *The Merchant of Venice* will keep on saying, much more powerfully, as long as Shakespeare endures.

9

THE TEMPEST
The Tragedy of Life

THE LAST play with which we shall deal in these chapters is *The Tempest,* generally accepted as the last play which Shakespeare wrote. It is the play in which the playwright consciously bade farewell to his creative art, as Prospero broke his staff and cast his magic book into a sea "deeper than did ever plummet sound."

Our previous plays have included tragedy, history, and comedy. But all have dealt with timeless issues of our mortal life. This play is, in general, a comedy—a particular kind of comedy called "romance"; but in truth it cannot be fitted into any category: it is unique.

It is, as it were, a play of memory, in which Shakespeare looks back over his whole career and summons for a curtain call the favorites of past scenes. His characters here are composites from a vast gallery of portraits adorning a score of previous plays. They are, therefore, perhaps less lifelike than the individuals from which they have been assembled, but more revealing of the types into which no single character can perfectly fit.

Shakespeare wrote *The Tempest* when he was at the very peak of his prestige and influence. He did not dwindle away, leaving his last writings an appendix in small print to vanished genius. As he peopled the stage for the last time, he was in the very exuberance of creative power, his mind a mint of jeweled phrases, his imagination an exchequer of fantasies awaiting his signature.

Because he had mastered the conventions, he could now transcend them. He could write as he liked, and he made full use of his freedom. *The Tempest,* therefore, is "of imagination all compact." It knows no limitation of chronology or geography; it owes no allegiance to time or space; it raises the curtain upon a supernatural and timeless world where Ariel can circle the earth in the twinkling of an eye, and a thousand years of kings and courts are to the essence of the drama no more than a watch in the night. Its setting can be as simple as that of Mr. Jed Harris' production of Thornton Wilder's play *Our Town,* where the audience is shown a signpost to Grover's Corners and left to imagine its local habitation in the earth, the universe, the mind of God.

One feature of the play is new. Hitherto, we have had to repeat monotonously that the material of the drama has been an old familiar tale told and retold before Shakespeare touched it with life and immortality. *The Tempest* is different. Obviously, the mind that conceived it did not work in a vacuum. Obviously, so simple a theme as a wreck at sea could not be new. Obviously, Shakespeare has stolen the realism of a storm-tossed ship from the mariners of England who themselves had discovered magic islands in far-off seas and had brought back tales of tropic worlds fit to kindle the imagination of a poet. A multitude of incidentals can be traced to a common reservoir of sixteenth-century knowledge. All this is inevitable; yet *The Tempest* has an indisputable originality. It may perhaps have sprung, like

Athena from the head of Zeus, full-fledged from the fancy of Shakespeare.

The Tempest opens with a storm. Shakespeare seems to have been fascinated by storms. He made thunder and lightning his stage properties. He overpowers his audience with raging nature in play after play—for example, *Julius Caesar, Macbeth, King Lear, Pericles, Cymbeline, Twelfth Night, The Comedy of Errors.* He made the storm a trademark of his craftsmanship. He used the storm because he knew the heart of man, and understood the immortal fascination which the storm exercises through the glamour of excitement and fear.

Other writers, of course, have fallen under the dread and spell of tempests. A few years before Shakespeare wrote his play, Bacon in his essay on truth declared, "It is a pleasure to stand upon the shore and see ships tossed upon the sea." [1] Dante in his *Inferno* has terrible earthquakes, gales, and torrents. Milton in his *Paradise Lost* has fallen angels overwhelmed with floods and "whirlwinds of tempestuous fire." The Bible has the Flood as the most terrible act of God.

But no great writer has loved the storm more than Shakespeare, and in *The Tempest* particularly he summons its potent aid. He employs it to give the emotional atmosphere at the start, as though he used a flash of lightning to throw a vivid glimpse on a scene of horror. He makes the opening moments convey impressive intimation of puny man amid the terrors of natural existence. With deft suggestion he manages to let us see the little ship tossed by tumultuous waves, hear the roar of the thunder, and feel the fury of overpowering gales. He touches the raging elements with augury of tempestuous evil about to break upon us; and perchance even with suggestion of the

---

[1] *Op. cit.,* p. 4.

little ships of our own lives in the storm-tossed voyage to eternity.

The tempest, however, is invoked not simply for effect. It has a journeyman purpose. It divides father from son, and brother from brother. It is a nemesis for past iniquities. The storm has a real part in *The Tempest,* as the Prince of Denmark has a part in *Hamlet.*

Yet the winds and the waves hear their Creator's word, "Thus far shalt thou go and no farther." And when calm has come to the place of violence, the storm in this play, as in other Shakespearean plays, is seen to be harmless. The characters are not victims of the tempest; they are victims of themselves.

The storm too brings in its completeness another Shakespearean pattern, the alternation of storm and music. One could write a thesis on that theme, and no doubt someone has. After the wind, after the fire, comes the still small voice of "marvellous sweet music." We learn that "the isle is full of noises, sounds and sweet airs, that give delight, and hurt not,"—as though the march of man were from chaos and storm to peace and harmony; and as though the harmonies of earth were but sympathetic echoes of the vaster harmonies of heaven. We remember the fancy of Lorenzo in *The Merchant of Venice,*

> Look how the floor of heaven
> Is thick inlaid with patines of bright gold:
> There's not the smallest orb which thou behold'st
> But in his motion like an angel sings,
> Still quiring to the young-eyed cherubins;
> Such harmony is in immortal souls;
> But whilst this muddy vesture of decay
> Doth grossly close it in, we cannot hear it.

In *The Tempest* finally we hear it. *The Tempest* is dominated by sound rather than sight.

THE TEMPEST: *The Tragedy of Life*

Because *The Tempest* is timeless, it can be kept to the unities of time. Save for one play, *The Comedy of Errors,* it is the shortest of all Shakespearean plays; yet it has finished symmetry of form and a clear framework of structure. More significant, the entire action, which in other plays sometimes extends to years, takes place in four hours. It is the story of a single afternoon which brings to human life a blaze of light like that which shone upon Saul on the road to Damascus.

The story itself is pure fantasy. We see it only as a symbol. We read it as we might read *Pilgrim's Progress* or the book of Revelation. The island is as far from reality, and as near to it, as the city of Mansoul; and the characters are of the same company as the Four Horsemen of the Apocalypse. Always between the spectator and the stage is a baffling curtain of gauze fashioned from "such stuff as dreams are made on." We look upon it distantly through a cloud of "thick-coming fancies."

The outline of the story is as follows: Prospero, duke of Milan, is a kind of philosopher-king who is more philosopher than king, and who prefers the study of nature's secrets to the administration of routine affairs of state. Shortly he is deposed by his treacherous brother, Antonio, who is aided by Alonso, king of Naples. With his three-year-old daughter Prospero is set adrift at sea in an open boat. He is saved from death by the kindness of a decent counselor, Gonzalo, who surreptitiously stocks the boat with "rich garments, linens, stuffs and necessaries," and also with Prospero's books of magic.

In time the castaways reach a desert island inhabited only by a misshapen monster named Caliban, son of the witch Sycorax. Prospero teaches Caliban to obey his will and do menial labor. He also releases a good spirit, Ariel, who has been imprisoned by Sycorax and who now becomes the magic agent of Prospero's purposes.

Spiritual Values in SHAKESPEARE

Twelve years later comes the tempest which provides the material of the play. Miranda is now a young woman, needless to say of surpassing beauty. She sees a ship battered by sea and gale and aflame with tongues of lightning, and she learns from her father that it is full of human beings, like herself, who will all find refuge upon the island. At the command of Prospero, Ariel besets the ship terribly with tempest; but he also contrives that the stricken passengers all survive—though scattered on different sections of the coast—and that the ship, with rent cordage and shattered deck, drifts at last into safe harbor where the mariners (having no further usefulness in the play) are, by spell of magic, put to sleep.

Few will find it difficult to anticipate that the victims of the tempest are Prospero's evil brother, Antonio, and his fellow conspirator, Alonso, king of Naples. Alonso is now in deep sorrow because he believes that the storm which he has survived has taken his son Ferdinand—who, in turn, elsewhere on the island, believes that his father and all the others are lost. Quicker than a girl today could arrange a date for Saturday night, Miranda comes across the young prince Ferdinand. Apart from her father, she has no memory of any man; but she has all the right reactions. And Ferdinand, although he has had his princely share of sweethearts, is willing to drop the memory of them all into a void to make way for this island goddess. In fact, love at first sight is so manifest that Prospero with his maturer wisdom says,

> This swift business
> I must uneasy make, lest too light winning
> Make the prize light.

He pretends to suspect Ferdinand and harshly sentences him to slave labor carrying heavy logs.

126

Meanwhile, in another part of the island Ferdinand's father, the rascally king of Naples, continues to mourn for Ferdinand and is comforted by the same good counselor, Gonzalo, who put the provisions in Prospero's boat. Ariel with his magic art now sends the castaways to sleep; and while they sleep, Prospero's brother, Antonio, former partner of the king's iniquity, plans to kill both the king and his counselor. Ariel intervenes by waking the sleepers, then tantalizes the whole company with mirages of sumptuous banquets spread before their eyes.

Still elsewhere, two "lewd fellows of the baser sort," Stephano, a drunken butler, and Trinculo, a jester, find a cask of wine that has floated ashore, and proceed to get drunk. They meet Caliban, get him drinking, and then plot with him to kill Prospero and take for themselves the island, not forgetting the lovely Miranda.

By this time it is midafternoon. It was two o'clock when the wreck was first seen; but all is in a land of fancy which transcends the limits of time. Ferdinand, much faster than Jacob, who served fourteen years for Rachel, has already finished his ordeal; and Prospero is preparing a magic banquet to celebrate the betrothal of Miranda.

As the silken threads of fantasy begin to complete their pattern, Ariel guides the guilty wanderers to Prospero, who recalls to them their wickedness, and then discloses to them his identity and explains his power. Yet Prospero ends by tempering justice with the quality of mercy. He grants forgiveness to all and restores to the king the lost Ferdinand. Finally Prospero takes the whole party on board the refitted ship and charges Ariel to bring them all in "calm seas, auspicious gales" back to Naples, where Miranda is to find her "brave new world." As a reward, Prospero frees Ariel from his service, and thus leaves the magic island as it was when he first landed: a lovely and lonely paradise, in sole possession of the brute monster Caliban. Prospero buries his wand and renounces the magic art of his lonely isle to live in the strength that is his own.

The Tempest was written in the year 1611, the year in which the King James translation first appeared, and from that time to this men have exercised their wits trying, like the Chaldean soothsayers, to read the interpretation thereof. Three centuries have not shown the way to any clear agreement, so it is not likely that I shall herewith settle the matter; and, fortunately, it is not necessary. Without waiting upon definitive interpretation, we can agree that the play has infinite scope of suggestion; and the suggestions that we find need not deny the validity of different suggestions. As we look upon a mountain from different vantage points, we see different views; so it is as we look at *The Tempest.*

The play is generally accepted as allegorical. An allegory, says the dictionary, is a prolonged metaphor in which a series of actions are symbolic of other actions and the characters are types or personifications. By this definition *The Tempest* can be taken as an allegory. But it is an allegory of an uncommon sort. *Pilgrim's Progress* is an allegory. But in it Christian and Giant Despair, Doubting Castle and the Slough of Despond, have a clarity of reference equaled only by their simplicity. Spenser's *Faery Queen,* published twenty years before *The Tempest,* is an allegory. But in it the Faery Queen is clearly Glory in the abstract and Queen Elizabeth in particular; her twelve knights are twelve virtues, such as Temperance, Chastity, Justice, Courtesy; and the Red Knight of Holiness is clearly the Anglican Church protecting the virgin Una, who is, just as clearly, the one true religion.

The Tempest is not so easily analyzed. Manifestly it contains more than appears on the surface. Manifestly it is alive with symbolic interpretation. The reader finds, as Ferdinand did, that "this is no mortal business." But those who have been dogmatic in interpretation have been distinguished more by vigor of assertion than by force of argument. A common suggestion is that Prospero represents the mind, Caliban the body, and Ariel the spirit. Another, coming from Ernest Renan, is that Prospero is Aristocracy; Caliban, Democracy; and Ariel, Religion. Still another is that Prospero represents Science, dominating nature through the discovery of her secrets; but that is to transform Shakespeare into a kind of Bacon—reversing the usual process.

One interesting modern study [2] says that *The Tempest* is a religious drama of the type of early religious mystery plays from which the art of the theater developed; and that, as such, it is an allegorical account of those inward experiences with which mystics have struggled from the darkness of sin and error into the light of wisdom and truth. In this reading Prospero is the Divine Spirit of Creation; Caliban is the Devil; Ariel, the Angel of the Lord, Miranda, the Celestial Bride. Of the other characters the comedians are led by the Devil; the court party reaches Purgatory; and Ferdinand attains Paradise.

This reading, however unconvincing, is not just an idle fancy. It comes from a mature study done with great care, and closely documented. (Notice that in one of these interpretations Caliban is seen as the Devil, in another he is seen as Democracy, and that both suggestions have merit.) The truth is, as Mark van Doren has observed, that any set of symbols moved close to

---

[2] Colin Street, *Shakespeare's Mystery Play* (London: Cecil Palmer, 1921).

this play lights up as in an electric field. "Its meaning in other words is precisely as rich as the human mind." [3]

All we can say is that just as the story of the prodigal son is more than the story of a man and a boy, so *The Tempest,* the final product of the greatest of all dramatists, is more than just an aimless fancy as beautiful and meaningless as the frost pattern on a windowpane. True, the playwright's project was not to preach but to please; yet he was not just blowing soap bubbles. He designed *The Tempest,* as he designed all his plays, to entertain; but he could entertain with ideas profound in meaning. The play is his reflection upon life and, therefore, in its own way sets forth his ultimate philosophy.

Most interpreters agree in finding the essence of the play set forth in three characters: Prospero, Ariel, Caliban. Prospero is, of course, Shakespeare himself, taking farewell of the world and of the people by whom he had been so fascinated—and especially of that "moving row of magic shadow shapes," that his "so potent art" had summoned to the stage. As he created Caliban and Ariel, he may have smiled to himself to think that the phantoms dancing in his brain would outlive the passing things of the outer world, the swords of warriors and the crowns of kings, the "cloud-capped towers, the gorgeous palaces." He looked upon the world of his creation, and, like the first Creator, he found it good.

Prospero, however, is more than Shakespeare. He is indeed Protean in character; and Proteus, we may recall, was a god who when seized would assume different shapes to escape prophesying. Prospero is in some ways the last of those medieval enchanters, such as Merlin and Vergil, who controlled the

[3] Mark van Doren, *Shakespeare* (London: George Allen & Unwin, 1941), p. 323.

powers of nature. He is in part a creator, more so than Oberon, king of the fairies in *A Midsummer-Night's Dream*. He has power as fate or destiny. He is a kind of subordinate Providence. At least he is the god of the island, and significantly he exercises his power to bring good out of evil. His magic art controls the elements of nature and also the souls of men; and he works his will to show us how human life should best be led.

Prospero is lord of the island. Hence, he may be man in nature. No other Shakespearean play has so much of the earthly, of the natural objects of the world. The island is a place where "every prospect pleases." Apparently, Shakespeare let his mind play upon the idea that later tempted Rousseau and men of our own time, the fancy that the right circumstance will produce the right people. The good counselor of the play, Gonzalo, who is well-meaning, but who, like Brutus, is too naïve about man's goodness, imagines that if he could live in such an island, he could create a paradise. If he were king, he muses, he would create here a commonwealth where all the bounties of nature would come without sweat or endeavor; where there would be no sword or gun, no law or class distinction, and no profit motive; where men and women, "idle . . . innocent and pure," would attain such perfection as to "excell the golden age." Gonzalo is rudely to be reminded that goodness is not so easily achieved. He wants no class distinction, and yet "he would be king." He fancies that in such a place all would live in equal content, but he is not asleep before his two companions are plotting to kill him that they may grasp the sovereignty. And he is awakened by bellowings as of lions and bulls, symbolic of the eternal beasts he must fight in nature and in man.

If Prospero suggests man's godlike power, Caliban suggests man's kinship with the brute. Caliban is not a pleasant addition to the stage, but he is not intended to be pleasant. He is the essence of grossness, an ugly puppy-headed monster, more than animal but less than man. He shows that he can learn the names of sun and moon and move into the world of thinking things. But he lacks moral sense. And he can profit by the education which Prospero began to give him only by gaining more knowledge with no more conscience, and becoming, therefore, more dangerous as he becomes more enlightened.

When Stephano gives him wine, Caliban is willing to become Stephano's slave; and he foments a plot to murder and to supplant Prospero. But he is reinforced with a certain low cunning. Himself illiterate, talking to illiterate men, he yet knows enough to realize that such as they cannot cope with Prospero unless they destroy his books. Caliban is tempted by Stephano's promise that when Prospero is destroyed, he, Caliban, will be lieutenant and viceroy. But he does not know that he is merely a tool to be cast aside as soon as he is used. At the end when the revolution has failed, he understands that he has been duped. In chagrin he exclaims,

> What a thrice-double ass
> Was I, to take this drunkard for a god,
> And worship this dull fool!

Browning speaks of "finished and finite clods, untroubled by spark"; [4] but Caliban has the spark. Browning himself in his poem "Caliban upon Setebos" imagines the dull monster reaching out for something beyond his native wickedness. Shakespeare pictures him as coming at last to penitence. At the end Caliban petitions for pardon, "I'll be wise hereafter, and seek for grace."

How much satire Shakespeare intended upon stupid people

---

[4] "Rabbi Ben Ezra."

—such as Jack Cade, revolutionist of the previous century—
who are led into wickedness by schemers with evil hearts, it is
difficult to say. Manifestly, however, Caliban typifies the beast-
liness in human nature.

Ariel, like Caliban, is symbolic. If Caliban is less than human,
Ariel is more. He is something like the earth spirit in Shelley's
Prometheus. He is free from mortal bounds. He has limitless
range of activity. He is a nymph of the sea, an angel of judgment, a minister of fate. He is fire or sound or spirit, tempest or
music. He is as inexhaustible as poetry or nature. He is beyond
humanity. He has no human feelings, though he imagines that
were he human, he could weep at sorrow. He is the ghost of an
idea.

Caliban and Ariel, as it were, extend the sweep of *The Tempest* to infinity. Other characters represent the people whom
Shakespeare has previously presented upon the stage: the kings
and nobles, evil and good; the young lovers; the base rascals "fit
for treasons, stratagems and spoils." Now beneath them all is
Caliban, and above them all is Ariel. Shakespeare is accentuat-
ing what he has previously said, that man is a being holding
large discourse.

What then is *The Tempest's* reading of life? What do we
see when Prospero gathers his projects to a head? We find ourselves in an atmosphere different from the tragedies, for we
come at last not to retribution and death but to mercy and forgiveness. We even have some grappling with the problem of evil
and its place in the universe. When Miranda asks her father
whether it was foul play or blessed mercy that visited their mis-
fortune upon them, he replies, "Both, both my girl." In Shakespeare's universe suffering has found a redemptive place. Even

the struggle against wickedness opens for men a possibility such as could never come in a paradise of perfection.

In *Cymbeline,* written but a little earlier, the mysterious voice of a god speaks to a sinful man, "Whom best I love, I cross." In *The Tempest* this idea is further developed. The godlike Prospero lays burdens on those he desires to redeem. Seemingly irrational in his sternness, he inflicts distress upon his own daughter that she might learn the greater value of her gifts. He visits with frightening threat the innocent old man Gonzalo, who fancies himself in a world of perfection. And the others—the sinning usurpers and the coarse, lustful men—he fills "brimful of sorrow and dismay." Yet all the time they are being prepared for pardon. Shakespeare was, in fact, expressing a philosophy written in one of his sonnets:

> Now I find true
> That better is by evil still made better;
> And ruin'd love, when it is built anew,
> Grows fairer than at first, more strong, far greater
> So I return rebuked to my content,
> And gain by ill thrice more than I have spent.
> (Sonnet CXIX)

We may say, then, that Shakespeare, taking his leave of the stage and of life itself, has found his way through the turmoil of the years, and through all the bitter experience that has laid its shadow upon his life, to a sympathy and tolerance that at first he did not know. This mature tolerance is based not upon indifference to evil but upon understanding. Having suffered wrong and felt resentment, he forgives the world his suffering and learns that in his forgiveness he has reached a new happiness and a new life.

In *The Merchant of Venice* he has already spoken his passage on mercy:

The quality of mercy is not strain'd,
It droppeth as the gentle rain from heaven
Upon the place beneath: it is twice blest;
It blesseth him that gives, and him that takes:
  'Tis mightiest in the mightiest: it becomes
The throned monarch better than his crown;
His sceptre shows the force of temporal power,
The attribute to awe and majesty,
Wherein doth sit the dread and fear of kings;
But mercy is above this sceptred sway;
It is enthroned in the hearts of kings,
It is an attribute to God himself;
And earthly power doth then show likest God's
When mercy seasons justice.

                                 (Act IV, scene 1)

In this last play Shakespeare has advanced to a further position. In a development of movement alien to the thinking of his earlier plays, he moves not only from justice to mercy but also from mercy to forgiveness. Prospero says of his enemies,

> They being penitent,
> The sole drift of my purpose doth extend
> Not a frown further.

Even to his treacherous brother he says, "I do forgive thy rankest fault." He finds that his "nobler reason" takes part against his fury and that "the rarer action is in virtue than in vengeance."

Shakespeare, that is, comes in this play not to retribution and death but to mercy and forgiveness. His voice is not disguised when in the epilogue he speaks through Prospero:

> My ending is despair,
> Unless I be relieved by prayer,
> Which pierces so, that it assaults

135

Mercy itself, and frees all faults.
As you from crimes would pardon'd be
Let your indulgence set me free.

Earlier in his plays he has stated in cold detachment, "The wages of sin is death." Where else, save in this final play, does he bring the conclusion of the whole matter to this elemental prayer. "Forgive us our trespasses, as we forgive them that trespass against us"?

10

THE INDIVIDUAL
AND THE ETERNITIES

IN THESE chapters we have dealt with a representative selection of Shakespeare's plays. We have sought not particularly their dramatic or poetic values but their spiritual values, and we have tried to see wherein these values bring illumination to the eternal laws of God.

The plays with which we dealt were four tragedies, *Hamlet, Othello, King Lear,* and *Macbeth;* two histories, *Richard III* and *Julius Caesar;* and two comedies, *The Merchant of Venice* and *The Tempest.* The latter comedy is of a particular type called a romance. That is to say, a "fictitious and wonderful tale" in which the interest lies not so much in the depiction or analysis of real life as in surprising incident or synthetic adventure.

Not to mention minor classifications, however, every schoolboy knows the classic division of Shakespeare's plays into comedies, histories, and tragedies. Though we must not be too subservient to a pattern, perhaps in a general way we may properly say that the comedies deal largely with the surface of life, taking infinite delight in its beauty, its wonder, and its joy, though always conscious that laughter lies not far from tears and that beauty comes soon to ashes.

137

Similarly, in a general way we may say that the histories deal with the life of energy and action, that their scope is limited by events and must conform to the chronicle of what has been. Even in the histories, however, we are conscious of the sure working of laws of retribution, the nemesis of evil-doing, and the presence of a moral order. We watch the curtain fall, sure that righteousness exalteth a nation and that sin is a reproach to any people.

In the tragedies, supremely, we see the human soul as the battleground of heaven and hell. In the tragedies shines the most intense realization of the glories that crown our human life, the passions that brighten or darken it, the infinite complexities that involve it, and the insoluble mystery that surrounds it. The essential quality in tragedy is what the Greeks called "catharsis," a purification of the emotions through pity or fear. Mr. C. E. Montague has written: "Tragedy is a peculiar sense of the presence of someone else's pain, a sense, too, that quickens your wits; you are given a new range of experience, such as sufferings of your own sometimes bring, but no shock to numb you past using it." [1] Certainly, in the tragedies we get the most titanic conceptions of the nature of life, the complexities of character, and the conflicts of good and evil. In the tragedies the chief characters stand out like faces in a Rembrandt painting, the revelation of a soul surrounded by the darkness and mystery of life.

The greatness of the tragedies came not only because the dramatist was now reaching the full maturity of that genius which he had disciplined by writing fully two dozen plays. He had, we may remember, begun writing plays when he was in his twenties and had finished all his tragedies when he had just entered his forties. But in addition to that apprenticeship of

---

[1] *Seven Famous One Set Plays* (Harmondsworth: Penguin Books, Ltd.), p. 81.

genius served in his youthful playwriting, Shakespeare tackled the tragedies after coming through the stormy waters of great emotional crisis. We know too little to be dogmatic about the experiences that left their mark upon the darkest of his writings. The essence of his tragedy appears to be that he was betrayed by a trusted friend and forsaken by a woman of dark and passionate beauty. We catch the overtones in his sonnets, but we have nothing which would serve a psychologist as a case history. We suspect, however, that, as Sir Walter Raleigh has said: "Many a life has been wrecked on the tenth part of the accumulated suffering which finds a voice in the tragedies." [2]

The Tempest is our final warrant that Shakespeare emerged from his searing experience increased in mental stature, moral wisdom, and spiritual insight. He returned to his work with a mature calm of mind and a healthy attitude toward life, not bitter in spirit but wise and urbane, with the magnificent defiance later voiced by Robert Louis Stevenson: "I believe in an ultimate decency of things, Ay, and if I woke in hell, I should still believe it." [3] His own life, as some of the characters he created, illustrates that every period of storm and stress which does not overcome character enriches character.

We must be clear that in all his plays Shakespeare was a dramatist and not a moralist. It is wrong to say that the comedies are to entertain, the histories to inform, and the tragedies to teach. The truth is that on some occasions Shakespeare entertained with comedy, on other occasions he entertained with history, on still other occasions he entertained with tragedy; but on all occasions in the theater his object was to

---

[2] *Shakespeare* (London: Macmillan & Co., 1928), p. 212.
[3] John Kilman, *The Faith of Robert Louis Stevenson* (Edinburgh: Oliphant Anderson & Ferrier, 1903), p. 265.

entertain. His method was not to point a moral; it was to enrich our sympathies, to stimulate our moral nature, and then, as one dealing with mature minds, to invite our independent judgment. One sees an illuminating contrast between Browning and Shakespeare. Browning was concerned, as he put it, that his poetry would not be a substitute for a cheap cigar. "I must write poetry," he said, "and save my soul." [4] Shakespeare said, "My project . . . was to please."

Moreover, Shakespeare never presents any moral issue as simple and clear. With him every moral issue is complex and cloudy, because life is complex and cloudy. In Shakespeare no character is wholly innocent. Desdemona is perhaps the nearest to being the sweetheart of Shakespeare—and of his readers. She is probably reminiscent of the dark and lovely lady who had been his joy and his despair. Yet he pictures even her in a situation too involved for complete innocence and shows her judging it wise to tell her husband what is convenient rather than what is true. In the original version of *King Lear* which Shakespeare used, Lear was humble and good to begin with. Shakespeare made him at first proud and arrogant, and at last purified through suffering.

As no character is wholly good, no character is wholly bad. Even Richard the Third, like Milton's Satan, has "th' unconquerable will . . . and courage never to submit or yield." Iago has some traits that excite our admiration. Regan and Goneril, the two women who were the worst of Shakespeare's females, are not wholly without excuse; and Regan is not as bad as Goneril. Shylock is not, as in the original material Shakespeare used, a villain without modification. Even in his villainy he embodies an ultimate appeal for humanity. Shakespeare paints

[4] Wm. Lyon Phelps, *Robert Browning* (Indianapolis: The Bobbs Merrill Co., 1932) , p. 60.

with darkly glowing tints but never in black or white, always in varying intensities of sepia. Mariana in *Measure for Measure* says:

> They say, best men are moulded out of faults,
> And, for the most, become much more the better
> For being a little bad.

And Henry the Fifth contrariwise says:

> There is some soul of goodness in things evil,
> Would men observingly distil it out.

We feel in the presence of Shakespeare's plays something as men must have done when Jesus presented the woman of the street and said: "He that is without sin . . . let him first cast a stone." There is always some barrier to complete condemnation; and, as in the rich young ruler, there is alway some barrier to complete approval. Indeed, in Shakespeare even virtue and vice themselves are not absolutes. The choice is never between one course absolutely good and another absolutely bad; the choice is, as it is in life, between one course, good but involved in evil, and another course, evil but embodying good.

Hence it is that some readers impatiently say that Shakespeare's plays have no morality whatever. Samuel Johnson puts it bluntly that Shakespeare writes without moral purpose. The moral worth in Shakespeare, however, is found not by reducing the complexities of life to a simplicity of choice, given in the comics, between the good guys and the bad guys—a simplicity which life does not often present. The moral worth is found, rather, in the underlying assumptions of the dilemmas which the plays present. Let me list three of these assumptions which become apparent as one reads the plays reflectively.

The first of these assumptions—and how we need it in this day of the totalitarian state—is that *individuals matter*. The plays are symphonies with variations on the theme of the eighth psalm: "What a being is man that Thou art mindful of him. Thou hast crowned him with glory and honour and made him but little lower than the angels." One cannot find proof texts for this thesis in the utterances of individuals. Hamlet says, "What a piece of work is man! how noble in reason! how infinite in faculty! . . . in action how like an angel! in apprehension how like a god!" Macbeth on the other hand says that life

> is a tale
> Told by an idiot, full of sound and fury,
> Signifying nothing.

One can always get contradictions in the varying speeches of Shakespeare's characters, because the speeches are all in character.

But if one turns from the spoken part to the assumptions on which the play proceeds, it becomes unmistakable that the chief worth is in individuals. Even in the histories Shakespeare is not concerned with history—the history is simply a stage for the study of personality. And in the tragedies the stories are incidental; they are borrowed and adapted; they are simply a platform on which the dramatist can present people.

Certain critics have complained that Shakespeare has no social sympathies, no thought of any kind of ideal society, no dream of any utopia, nor, certainly, of any kingdom of God; and the critics are not without justification. Shakespeare saw all social evils and excellencies rooted in individuals. He saw the tragedy of England traced in the corrupting passions of evil men. He saw the desolation of Scotland written in the iniquity of Macbeth. He saw that in Denmark the times were "out of joint" because one man had sinned. He saw Romeo and Juliet brought to calamity and untimely death because of a feud between the Montagues and the Capulets. He saw all social good and evil as but the overflow of individual souls. He brings us back, to a certain extent, to the atmosphere of the parables, which are stories of individuals: the shepherd with the lost sheep, the woman with the lost coin, and the father with the wayward son. One could even say with fitting reverence that Shakespeare was akin to Christ in finding the focal point of interest in the human soul.

One might present a significant illustration in Shakespeare's treatment of women. The place accorded to women in his plays is almost as astonishing as the place given to them in the New Testament. We do not realize the wonder of either until we compare them with contemporary thinking. In Shakespeare's day the stage was too filthy to permit women to be present. No actress ever appeared on any stage. Female characters were played by boys in woman's dress. Yet what could be more surprising than the gallery of Shakespeare's women? They were, to be sure, women and not angels, creatures "not too bright nor good for human nature's daily food." Some of them also were evil. Cleopatra remained for Shakespeare, as for Antony, the serpent of old Nile. But Cleopatra, significantly, was the only one whose life was limited to the sensuous. The others—Lady Macbeth, Goneril, Regan, Ophelia, Desdemona, all their train —help to maintain the constant theme that women, when good, are the biggest influence in man's life, and, when bad, bring woe to the world.

Significantly, Shakespeare painted his loveliest portraits after his bitter experience. Desdemona in *Othello*, Cordelia in *King Lear*, Imogen in *Cymbeline*, and Miranda in *The Tempest* are lovelier and nobler women than he drew in the days of his youth. In his estimate of women Shakespeare was not a child of the

Renaissance; he was nearer to being a child of the New Testament.

Whether male or female, whether good or bad, the characters in Shakespeare's plays are rarely contemptible. Schiller, it is said, could write only in a room redolent with the smell of decaying apples. Shakespeare has no smell of rottenness. He parades no incest, sex perversion, abortion, depraved children, or other specimens of putridness which in the present generation pass for realism. Shakespeare has none of the bitter pessimism which prompted Mark Twain to suggest as the title for one of his unpublished works *Thirty Thousand Years Among the Microbes by a Microbe.* Shakespeare watched human follies and absurdities. He knew the depths to which human beings can sink. After the fashion, though far behind the penetration, of Christ, he knew what was in man. But in all the gloom and iniquity he kept alive a belief in human power and greatness. Somebow, even in the darkest scenes he makes the soul shine forth like a morning star.

Moreover, in Shakespeare the characters that are admirable, both men and women, are more numerous than the characters who are base. Altogether Shakespeare's plays are a picture gallery of 250 individual characters, and to see them all is to feel that the world is a place to meet fine people and many of them. We can say with Miranda:

> How many goodly creatures are there here!
> How beauteous mankind is! O brave new world,
> That has such people in't!

We leave his plays, thinking not in the temper of Macbeth that man is a fool on his way to dusty death, but more in the temper of the book of Genesis: God saw the world, and it was good. The primary assumption of all Shakespearean drama is that individuals matter. In a day when the individual is expendable, our spirits can welcome the reinforcement of that classic insight.

The second assumption underlying all the plays is that *individuals are responsible*. Man is the architect of his own fate. He works out his own salvation.

The Greek plays were pervaded by fatalism; blind necessity used men as pawns and controlled even the gods. Man was tricked by fate, constrained by powers vaster than himself, and powerless to change his destiny.

In Shakespeare circumstance has a part. Sometimes, indeed, man seems like the plaything of chance. Desdemona drops a handkerchief; Juliet arrives just too late to save Romeo; Edgar comes just too late to save Cordelia. Circumstance and the hazards of chance have their part in drama because they have their part in life, and Shakespeare is too clear-eyed to deny it.

But in Shakespeare circumstance and chance play only a part. Man is never doomed by these alone. He is never ruined in independence of his own character. When all the chances are accounted for, Othello is stupid in his doubt of Desdemona; Macbeth is guilty of harboring evil ambitions; Lear is more foolish than his fool; Richard the Third is responsible for choosing iniquity; Brutus is ruined by his own stupidity. The grimmest conflict man has is not with some outward fate but with himself. As George Meredith put it:

> Passions spin the plot:
> We are betrayed by what is false within.

Augustine in his confessions tells how once with a pack of riotous companions he raided an orchard and stripped a pear tree. "I resolved to steal," he says, "and I did steal, not from any pressure of want and penury but from the scorn of justice and the full-fledged insolence of sin." [5] Shakespeare never forgets what Augustine calls "the full-fledged insolence of sin." He presents men not as the creatures of circumstance but as the creators of circumstance. When he has set up his environment and paraded his circumstance, he makes it clear that, after all, human action is the central fact in tragedy and the main cause of catastrophe. He tells us that what is important is not where we are, but what we are. He sends us out from the plays feeling not helpless but rather awed, pitiful, and reverent, and knowing that the issues of life are in the heart. "The fault, dear Brutus, is not in our stars, but in ourselves."

The third assumption is equally fundamental: individuals, free and responsible, are *living in a moral order.*

What Shakespeare does to create a tragedy is to take an old story and give it an entirely new content; and this content is moral complexity. An authoritative critic of Shakespeare maintains that, except in a few scenes in *A Midsummer-Night's Dream,* there are not thirty consecutive lines in Shakespeare that do not rely upon the vocabulary of ethics or relate in some way to standards of conduct or choices between right and wrong. He points out that Shakespeare omitted from the original material of his plays an immense amount of filth and licentiousness, and he declares that a writer shows his moral bias by what he avoids as well as by what he includes. The critic further points out that everywhere throughout Shakespeare's plays evil ruins and wrecks and destroys, that everywhere evil is the source of disorder. He concludes by saying that for Shakespeare to work on a plot meant inevitably to inoculate it with moral notions.

All this has unacknowledged indebtedness to the Scriptures.

[5] Quoted in W. M. Macgregor, *The Making of a Preacher* (Philadelphia: Westminster Press, 1946), p. 54.

The lineage of Shakespeare's thinking goes back in most cases not to the poets of Greece but to the prophets of Israel. Dean Farrar said that the grandeur of Shakespeare's genius makes some of the deepest truths of scripture glow with new brightness and intensity. One might take a general text for all Shakespeare's tragedies: "Be not deceived; God is not mocked: for whatsoever a man soweth, that shall he also reap."

Yet the plays have one conspicuous lack. Nowhere have they suggestion of any *power to redeem*. They are a running commentary on the theme that the wages of sin is death, but nowhere do they add that the gift of God is eternal life. In this particular Shakespeare is infinitely different from Jesus Christ. Christ looked upon men and women with limitless faith. He saw the woman of the street, the hated publican, the thief on the cross—these and many others—not with condemnation but with hope. He said to Peter, "Thou art Simon . . . thou shalt be called Cephas . . . A stone." He saw persons, not as they were, but as they might be.

Shakespeare had no such vision. He saw men as they were—no more, no less. He felt no responsibility whatever for what they might be. He was no evangelist. He was but an observer. He found equal interest in a man who gave himself to the devil and one who chose to follow his better nature. He could have said as he surveyed their lives,

> "I sit as God holding no form of creed
> But contemplating all." [6]

Shakespeare nowhere lets us hear a call to repentance. Macbeth, Iago, Richard, Regan, Goneril, pass without halt to their doom. They grow harder and harder and in the end seem to have sold

[6] Alfred Lord Tennyson, "The Palace of Art."

themselves to the devil. Only the latest plays are touched with different thought. *King Lear* brings some suggestion of a path through suffering to redemption. *The Tempest* points the way from justice to mercy and from mercy to forgiveness. Only at the end do we catch some overtone of the evangel.

Shakespeare, then, is not the gospel, just as the Ten Commandments are not the gospel. Yet the Ten Commandments, though not the gospel, have validity within their limits; and Shakespeare, likewise, is never far from the eternal verities. He stands with Dante and with Milton among the great teachers of the race. As an aged Scottish minister a century ago advised an inquiring young ordinand, Shakespeare is one of the two companions necessary to the human mind. For Shakespeare tells you all you need to know about man, and the Bible tells you all you can know about God.

INDEX OF
SHAKESPEARE QUOTATIONS

149

Julius Caesar—*cont'd*

I	ii	139	145
I	ii	207	96
I	ii	241	91
II	i	189	97
II	ii	116	97
III	i	111	92
III	i	256	94
III	ii	88 ff.	96
III	ii	188	118
III	ii	265 ff.	98
IV	i	1 ff.	98
IV	iii	22	94
IV	iii	67 ff.	95
IV	iii	146	96
V	iii	94	102
V	v	68	95
V	v	69	95

KING JOHN

IV	iii	10	77
V	vii	112	77

KING LEAR

I	i	228	63
I	i	243	64
I	ii	20	65
I	iv	283	65
III	ii	58	62
III	iv	34	69
V	iii	7	70
V	iii	20	70
V	iii	233	68
V	iii	258	71
V	iii	274	63
V	iii	292	68

MACBETH

I	ii	1	53
I	ii	17 ff.	53
I	iii	65	49
I	iv	50	58
I	v	1	59
I	v	18	58
I	v	71	58
I	vii	72	56
II	i	42	58

Macbeth—*cont'd*

II	iii	98	59
II	iii	119	71
III	ii	22	59
III	ii	50	48
IV	i	48	53
IV	i	79	51
V	i	18	54
V	i	36	54
V	i	38-39	55
V	i	42	53
V	i	56	55
V	i	86	52
V	iii	38	125
V	v	23	59
V	v	26	142
V	v	35	52
V	vii	15	52
V	viii	98	56

MEASURE FOR MEASURE

V	i	440	141

MERCHANT OF VENICE

I	iii	126 ff.	107
I	iii	146	107
II	vii	16	108
II	vii	37	107
II	ix	50	107
III	i	62	116
IV	i	90	116
IV	i	184	135
IV	i	263	109
IV	i	304	109
IV	i	331	109
IV	i	332	117
IV	i	388	109
V	i	1	111
V	i	58	124
V	i	85	133

MIDSUMMER NIGHT'S DREAM

V	i	8	122

OTHELLO

I	iii	94	38
I	iii	158	41

INDEX OF PERSONS AND SUBJECTS